Sexual Violence

About the Author

William R. Holcomb, PhD, ABPP, MBA, has been a forensic psychologist for approximately 30 years. He received his doctorate from the University of Missouri-Columbia and later was awarded a diplomate certification of Forensic Psychology by the American Psychological Association. He has maintained an active clinical and consulting practice throughout his career. His primary areas of career focus have been competency, insanity, personal injury, and threat assessment evaluations and the treatment of criminal offenders in community, jail, and prison settings. He is currently a Professor and Program Director for Forensic Studies at Alliant International University in San Francisco, CA.

Advances in Psychotherapy – Evidence-Based Practice

Danny Wedding; PhD, MPH, Prof., St. Louis, MO
(Series Editor)
Larry Beutler; PhD, Prof., Palo Alto, CA
Kenneth E. Freedland; PhD, Prof., St. Louis, MO
Linda C. Sobell; PhD, ABPP, Prof., Ft. Lauderdale, FL
David A. Wolfe; PhD, Prof., Toronto
(Associate Editors)

The basic objective of this series is to provide therapists with practical, evidence-based treatment guidance for the most common disorders seen in clinical practice – and to do so in a "reader-friendly" manner. Each book in the series is both a compact "how-to-do" reference on a particular disorder for use by professional clinicians in their daily work, as well as an ideal educational resource for students and for practice-oriented continuing education.

The most important feature of the books is that they are practical and "reader-friendly:" All are structured similarly and all provide a compact and easy-to-follow guide to all aspects that are relevant in real-life practice. Tables, boxed clinical "pearls", marginal notes, and summary boxes assist orientation, while checklists provide tools for use in daily practice.

Sexual Violence

William R. Holcomb
Alliant International University, San Francisco, CA and Coalinga State
Hospital, CA

Library of Congress Cataloging in Publication

is available via the Library of Congress Marc Database under the
LC Control Number 2010921353

Library and Archives Canada Cataloguing in Publication

Holcomb, William R
    Sexual violence / William R. Holcomb.

(Advances in psychotherapy--evidence-based practice ; v. 17)
Includes bibliographical references.
ISBN 978-0-88937-333-4 :c$37.50

    1. Sex offenders--Psychology. 2. Sex offenders--Rehabilitation. 3. Violence in men.
I. Title. II. Series: Advances in psychotherapy--evidence-based practice ; v. 17

RC560.S47H642010   616.85'8306   C2010-900848-0

PUBLISHING OFFICES
USA: Hogrefe Publishing, 875 Massachusetts Avenue, 7th Floor, Cambridge, MA 02139
             Phone (866) 823-4726, Fax (617) 354-6875; E-mail customerservice@hogrefe-publishing.com
EUROPE: Hogrefe Publishing, Rohnsweg 25, 37085 Göttingen, Germany
             Phone +49 551 49609-0, Fax +49 551 49609-88, E-mail publishing@hogrefe.com

SALES & DISTRIBUTION
USA: Hogrefe Publishing, Customer Services Department,
             30 Amberwood Parkway, Ashland, OH 44805
             Phone (800) 228-3749, Fax (419) 281-6883, E-mail customerservice@hogrefe.com
EUROPE: Hogrefe Publishing, Rohnsweg 25, 37085 Göttingen, Germany
             Phone +49 551 49609-0, Fax +49 551 49609-88, E-mail publishing@hogrefe.com

OTHER OFFICES
CANADA: Hogrefe Publishing, 660 Eglinton Ave. East, Suite 119-514, Toronto, Ontario, M4G 2K2
SWITZERLAND: Hogrefe Publishing, Länggass-Strasse 76, CH-3000 Bern 9

Hogrefe Publishing
Incorporated and registered in the Commonwealth of Massachusetts, USA, and in Göttingen, Lower Saxony,
Germany

Printed and bound in the USA
ISBN: 978-0-88937-333-4

Acknowledgments

I want to thank my friend Danny Wedding, who convinced me to write this book and who provided supportive encouragement and valued editorial insight as this work took shape. Of course, this book would not be possible without all the clients I have had across 35 years of work as a therapist in private practice, hospitals, mental health centers, jails, and prisons. From them I have learned so much. I have also been very fortunate in having many wonderful supervisors and colleagues who have helped me become a better therapist and forensic psychologist.

Dedication

To my daughter, Megan, who is very wise and always a joy for her father. This book is also dedicated to all my friends and supportive colleagues at Alliant University.

Table of Contents

1

Description of the Problem

Sexual violence remains a significant problem in our society. Mental health professionals too often confront the immediate consequences of sexual assault in emergency rooms, victim support centers, correctional institutions, mental hospitals, and outpatient clinics. Law enforcement personnel and child protective agencies are persistently faced with child sexual molestation, incest, intimate partner sexual violence, and rape. The good news in this horrific story is that the prevalence of sexual assault seems to have been going down in the United States since the mid-1970s, according to the National Victimization Survey (Catalano, 2005), but the incidence remains high and a significant presenting problem for mental health professionals.

This book will present an overview of sexual violence as seen in many clinical settings, review key diagnostic guidelines, and assessment strategies, outline some of the current theories for understanding sexual violence, and then focus on effective treatment processes, and strategies. I will focus primarily on adult male perpetrators of sexual violence with both child and adult victims. Although there is growing awareness of female perpetrators (Schwartz & Cellini, 1995), the focus will primarily be on male perpetrators since males commit the vast majority of sexual violence incidents. Most important, I will use a broad definition of sexual violence to include not only the use of physical force, but sexual coercion utilizing position authority and verbal aggression. An important goal of this work will be to provide tools that mental health professionals can use in different institutional and community treatment settings to be more effective when working with perpetrators of sexual violence.

Another goal of this book will be to inform clinicians and the public with the most recent science on sexual violence. Unfortunately, there are many myths about sexual violence, and in particular sexual crimes, which are promoted by the monster archetype in our culture's unconscious. This book will review research that challenges some of these myths. Among these myths are that sex offenders cannot be treated, that most sex offenders are arrested and not in the community, that sex offenders are almost sure to commit other sex offenses if released, that pornography causes sexual violence, and that all sex offenders are psychopathic and narcissistic. I strongly believe informed clinicians can make better decisions about prevention and effective intervention with sexually violent individuals.

1.1   Definition

Sexual violence can be defined in several ways. We will use the definition of Lalumiere, Harris, Quinsey, and Rice (2005) who provide definitions of rape and of sexual coercion. Rape is defined as, "The forceful act of sexual intercourse against a person's will and/or any physical sexual contact performed with the use of threat or physical force" (p. 10). Sexual coercion is defined as, "Any physical sexual contact performed without a person's consent using any coercive methods (e.g., using a position of authority or verbal pressure)" (p. 10).

There have been some notable trends in official reports of rape crimes over the last few years that are supported by results from self-reported national survey data of victimization. Between 1982 and 1992, the prevalence of rape increased dramatically from 24 per 100,000 to 43 per 100,000. However, the rate of forcible rape then precipitously declined by 26% from 1992 to 2001 to a rate of 31 per 100,000. There was a more dramatic decrease of approximately 68% in victim-reported rapes in the National Crime Victimization Survey. The rate of rapes that were self-reported but that did not lead to arrest dropped from 250 per 100,000 in 1983 to approximately 54 per 100,000 in 2001 (Catalano, 2005). Confidence in this decrease in reported rapes is bolstered by the fact that during this same time there was a parallel drop in most criminal activities (Lalumiere et al., 2005).

The rate of reported rapes has decreased in the past decade to 31 per 100,000, but remains unacceptably high.

The number of sex crimes and self-reported victimizations not leading to arrest remains unacceptably high. Approximately 95,000 forcible rape crimes occurred in 2004 (US Department of Justice, 2006). The National Crime Victimization Survey reported that approximately 200,000 rapes were self-reported during this period (Catalano, 2005). The majority of sexual assault victims are minors and female (La Ford, 2005). In addition, the number of sex offenders in prisons has dramatically increased in recent years at a much faster rate than other kinds of offenders. Departments of correction are supervising over 240,000 sex offenders, with approximately half being supervised in the community at any one time (Greenfield, 1997; La Ford, 2005). These prevalence and incarceration rates clearly illustrate the tremendous costs to society in both human suffering and the expense associated with criminal justice intervention.

One of the assumptions of this book is that sexual violence occurs both in the commission of sex crimes that lead to arrests and in cases of violent and coercive behavior in the community in which arrests do not occur. Some of the settings in which arrests may not occur are date rape, intimate partner violence, and child sexual abuse. In 2005, seven out of ten female rape or sexual assault victims stated that the offender was an intimate, rather than a relative, friend, or acquaintance (Catalano, 2005). The prevalence of intimate partner sexual violence underscores the importance of understanding noncriminal or nonarrest sexual violence (Bennice & Resick, 2003). One national self-report survey found that 7.7% of women report being raped by their intimate partner (Tjaden & Thoennes, 1998, 2000). Another researcher estimated that between 10% and 14% of married women are raped by their partner (Russel, 1990). When questioned about why their intimate partners rape them, 78% of victims reported that their husbands needed to prove their manhood (Frieze, 1983). Others have reported that their partners felt they had an entitlement of sex or that their partners used sex to control them (Bergen & Bukovec, 2006). The perpetrators in this later study were in a court-ordered domestic violence treatment program. Of these individuals, 33% had white-collar jobs, 56% were married to or currently living with their partners, 84% admitted to physical acts of violence against their partners, and 40% indicated that their use of physical violence had been increasing.

7 out of 10 rape/ sexual assault victims are intimate partners of the offender.

It cannot be assumed that perpetrators of intimate partner violence are different from those arrested for sex crimes. Groth and Gary (1981) reported that marital rapists share a number of characteristics with incarcerated rapists, including prior histories of sexual violence, deficient communication skills, problems with emotional intimacy, and the view that refusal of sexual intimacy by their partners is intolerable. Intimate partner sexual violence is a prime example of a situation in which victimization occurs, but there is no arrest or criminal conviction.

A common setting in which sexual violence and its effects are all too often seen is in health clinics. In one study of 1401 adult women who attended a family practice clinic, 20% experienced intimate partner violence in current or recent relationships (Coker, Smith, McKeown, & King, 2000). Women who experienced both sexual and physical abuse had higher scores on a battering scale and a spousal abuse scale, which led the authors to suggest that sexual abuse could be a marker for severe violence and even violence escalation. Both the victims and the perpetrators in this study tended to be unemployed, suggesting to the authors that unemployment of the victim could be a sign of the extreme control exercised by the perpetrator of violence. Family violence often brings both partners and the children into contact with mental health professionals.

20% of women seen in health clinics report being victims of recent sexual violence.

1.2   Epidemiology

Establishing the true incidence and prevalence of sexual violence is difficult to determine because of the variations in definitions used in epidemiological surveys. Also, the under-reporting of victimization further contributes to inaccuracy of prevalence estimates of sexual violence. In one random selection survey in San Francisco, only 2% of incest offenses and 6% of child sexual victimization by nonfamily offenders were reported (Russel, 1990). Henry and McMahon (2000) estimate that 91% of cases of child sex abuse are unreported. Kilpatrick (1996) estimated that 56% of women who are sexually assaulted do not report the crime.

Approximately 9 out of 10 child sexual abuse incidents are not reported.

The prevalence of self-reported sexual violence in community samples is high. A quarter of college women report either being raped (15%) or resisting an attempted rape (12%) (Koss, Gidyez, & Wisniewski, 1987). Of a random sample of women in San Francisco, 44% indicated that they had been raped (Russel, 1990). Self-reported sex abuse as children also is high. Peters, Wyatt, and Finkelhor (1986) reviewed the literature and estimated rates of sex abuse for children at 34% for females and 17% for males.

56% of women who are sexually assaulted do not report the crime.

There is a continuum of sexual violence that can extend from sexual exploitation to sadistic sexual murder. Sexual exploitation can be expressed in many ways, but a frequent form is that of exhibitionism (Rabinowitz, Firestone, Bradford, & Greenberg, 2002). In one survey, 30% of women reported experiences with men who had exposed their genitalia (Divasto et. al, 1984). On the other end of the continuum of sexual violence are rape and child sex abuse, which remain two of the most devastating and common types of sexual violence.

An important method for collecting information about the prevalence of sexual violence comes from self-report community and college surveys where recipients are asked if they have committed violent sexual acts. Confidentiality is typically granted to the survey participant to help reduce response bias. Laumann, Gagnon, Michael, and Michaels (1994) found that 2.8% of adult males and 1.5% of adult females report that they had forced someone to have sex. Herman (1990) reported the astounding finding that between 4% and 17% of adult males self-report having molested a child. Malamuth (1989) reported that 15% of college males indicate that they have had some type of sexual contact with a child. Malamuth (1981) also found that 35% of college males indicated that they would commit rape if they were sure they would not be caught. These survey findings are surprisingly high given the assumption that because of positive response bias, recipients would be expected not to report sexually violent actions, even with confidentiality guaranteed.

35% of college males indicate that they would commit rape if they were sure they would not be caught.

The prevalence of sexual violence in the community is dramatized even more by the fact that perpetrators often have multiple victims. A remarkable study by Abel et al. (1987) granted immunity to incarcerated offenders and then asked them about the number of people they had victimized. Child molesting offenders ($n=252$), when granted confidentiality, admitted to 55,250 attempts at child molestation with 38,727 being successful. Rapists ($n=126$) reported having 882 victims and 142 exhibitionists exposed themselves on 71,696 occasions. Data from community samples of sexually coercive males who have never been arrested parallel these results (Lisak & Miller, 2002).

1.3   Effects of Sexual Violence on Victims

Effectively addressing sexual violence remains a priority because of the devastating short-term and long-term effects on victims. Conte and Schuerman (1987) have described the effects of child sexual abuse on victims. Among the short-term effects are loss of self-worth, emotional distress, nightmares or deep sleep problems, aggression, and problems concentrating. Among the long-term consequences are eating disorders, loss of sexual responsiveness, problematic sexual behaviors, personality disorders, and problems with emotional development. Burgess and Holmstrom (1974) have written about the devastating effects of rape that parallel posttraumatic stress symptoms. These effects include fear that can develop into full phobia, panic disorder, or generalized anxiety. Other symptoms include mood swings, social withdrawal, deteriorating work or school performance, substance use, and rejection of friends.

1.4 Sexual Coercion in the Community

Some have argued that descriptive data on community and college samples do not generalize to our understanding of criminal offenders (Stinson, Sales, & Becker, 2008). However, an arrest can be happenstance, and the circumstances contributing to sexual violence that leads to an arrest and to sexual violence that does not lead to an arrest may be similar. There would be more danger of missing important information if data from both community and incarcerated populations are not examined.

There are a number of similarities among different kinds of sexual coercive men. Lalumiere et al. (2005) describe similarities between incarcerated rapists and college students and community samples as "striking" (p. 78). Compared to nonincarcerated coercive males, rapists from prison and psychiatric hospitals tend to be more antisocial, more hostile, less empathic, have more favorable attitudes toward rape, and have more conservative attitudes toward women and sexuality.

There are important similarities between incarcerated sex offenders and sexually coercive males in the community.

There have been some follow-up studies of college males who have self-reported sexual violence. Gidycz, Warkentin, and Orchowski (2007) surveyed a convenience sample of 425 college undergraduates and surveyed the same group three months later. The Sexual Experiences Survey (Koss & Oros, 1982; Koss & Gidyez, 1985) was used to assess sexual aggression. Overall, 10.2% reported sexual aggression during the three-month follow-up with 4.4% reporting an actual contact that was sexually aggressive and 2.6% reporting rape or attempted rape. Of those reporting sexual aggression, 63% of the incidents involved alcohol use by the perpetrator, 57.1% of the incidents involved alcohol use by the victim, 54.3% of the incidents were in a dating relationship or on a causal date, and 42.8% of the incidents involved victims who were acquaintances. There was only one stranger victim. Those who had a history of sexual aggression were three times more likely to exhibit sexual aggression during the follow-up, and those with a history of verbal aggression toward partners had increased risk of sexual aggression. This close connection between sexual aggression and verbal aggression is important to note.

In a groundbreaking study of a national sample of college students (n=2,972), Koss et al. (1987) found that 15% of college students reported that, since the age of 14, they had raped or attempted rape. When comparing sexually coercive college males to noncoercive males who were sexually active, it was found that the coercive males tended to have stronger pro-rape attitudes, stronger adversarial sexual beliefs, more pronounced sex-role stereotypes, more acceptance of interpersonal violence, and more hostile beliefs toward women. This study also reported a three-month rape incidence rate of 3.7% and a one-year incidence rate of 4.5% by college males, when the definition of rape was limited to the legal definition of rape.

Approximately 15% of college males report committing rape or attempting rape.

White and Smith (2004) performed a five-year follow-up study of college male freshmen. At one university, 65% of all college freshmen males participated in the study. Unfortunately, only 22% completed all follow-up data collection across the five-year follow-up, so these results need to be replicated. The authors were attempting to evaluate earlier findings (Malamuth, Linz, Heavy, Barnes, & Acker, 1995) that experiencing family violence, including sexual abuse, contributed to victims later being sexually coercive toward women, along with delinquency and sexual promiscuity. Other data had revealed that approximately 24.4% of college males admit sexual aggression against women with 7.8% admitting to behavior that would meet the legal definition of rape (Koss, 1992). Overall, White and Smith (2004) found that 9.5% of the men were victims of sexual abuse and 30.7% had experienced either parental physical punishment or domestic violence. Around one-third (34.5%) reported perpetrating some type of sexual assault in the five-year follow-up period.

The White and Smith (2004) research is important because it identified factors that contributed to sexually coercive behavior during the five-year follow-up. There was a two-fold increase in perpetrating sexual assault given any kind of childhood victimization. A risk percentage was assigned based on type of childhood victimization experienced. Using survival analysis, it was found that the risk of sexual violence attributed to experiencing childhood sexual abuse was 5.7%, to witnessing domestic violence was 8.7%, and to experiencing parental physical punishment was 19.9%. The risk was 23% if all types of victimizations were included. If the perpetrated sexual violence of these college males was limited to just rape or attempted rape, then this risk increased to 37%. There appeared to be a group of males for whom the number of assaults increased into college. Adolescent perpetration of sexual violence did increase the likelihood that sexual victimization would occur in college, even though the number of perpetrators decreased across time, the number of assaults per perpetrator increased (White & Smith, 2004). This effort at completing research that specifically assigns risk probabilities to different types of early childhood victimization is important and instructive.

> **Given any history of childhood victimization, there is a two-fold increase in probability of committing sexual assault as an adult.**

Malamuth et al. (1995) completed another important 10-year follow-up study of college students. Data were collected for 132 of 423 original subjects. Interviews and videotapes were collected of the original subjects and their partners doing a problem-solving exercise 10 years after initial data collection. Remarkably, sexual coercion in the present, as reported in interviews with partners/spouses, correlated .41 with original sexual coerciveness data (using the Sexual Experiences Survey) collected 10 years earlier. In addition, nonsexual aggression directed to the partner during present problem-solving exercises correlated with earlier self-reported sexual coercion (.51) and current difficulties with marital distress and sexual problems (.38). Sexual coercion in the couple relationships was predicted by the number of early sex experiences and measured general hostility to women in the present.

Other studies have examined correlates of sexual coercion in community samples. Walker, Rowe, and Quinsey (1993) reported a high correlation between the Right Wing Authoritarianism Scale and measures of hostility to women, acceptance of interpersonal violence, adversarial sexual beliefs, rape myth acceptance scales, and a measure of past sexually coercive behavior and likelihood of future sexual coercion. In another correlation study, Carr and VanDeusen (2004) used the Sexual Experience Survey to determine levels of sexual coercion and then correlated those levels with a number of scales with 99 undergraduate history students. Sexual coercion correlated significantly with acceptance of rape myths (.43), acceptance of interpersonal violence (.46), beliefs about the adversarial nature of sexual behavior (.45), satisfaction with the typical sex roles of men and women (.37), and hostility toward women

> **Sexual violence is strongly correlated with attitudes of authoritarianism, acceptance of interpersonal violence, rape myths, and past sexual coercive behavior.**

(.28). Sexually coercive college men were also found to drink more alcohol, have had more sexual partners, and use more pornography. There was also a significant correlation between being sexually coercive on this survey and having been sexually abused, and/or witnessing family interpersonal violence.

Another study of noncriminal sexually assaultive behavior provides insight into the relationship of diagnoses, early child relationships, and trauma to later sexually coercive behavior (Quimette, 1997; Quimette & Riggs, 1998). College males who self-reported committing rape or attempted rape on the Sexual Experience Survey were compared to a sample of 57 who denied any sexual aggression, but were sexually active. Sexually aggressive behavior was associated with negative childhood experiences with fathers. These reports included the father being emotionally distant, having uncaring fathers, and witnessing their father being violent in the family. A structured diagnostic interview was also used (SCID; Spitzer, Williams, Gibbon, & First, 1987) that helped to determine impulse control problems during adolescence. It was found that having impulse control problems in adolescence also had an effect on later sexual aggression. Having delinquent peers, hostile attitudes toward women, and rigid sex-role beliefs predicted sexual aggression, but these factors did not mediate the connection between poor fathering and sexual aggression. This work is important in linking inadequate fathering to later sexual aggression. This finding has implications for designing interventions that can address the adult attachment deficiencies that may be present because of these early negative fathering influences (Burk & Burkhart, 2003).

> **Sexual aggression is associated with negative childhood experiences with fathers and emotional distancing from the father.**

Remarkably, college students in this study who self-reported sexual aggression in the form of either rape or attempted rape were found to have diagnoses quite similar to those found in an incarcerated sample (Quimette, 1997). These sexually aggressive college men met the criteria for conduct disorder ($p<.025$), alcohol abuse/dependence ($p<.007$), and drug abuse/dependence ($p<.025$) when compared to the nonaggressive males. These results underscore long-term difficulties with impulse control problems with these college males. Of the sexually aggressive men, 17% met criteria for conduct disorder compared to only 2% of the nonsexually aggressive men; these men were two to three times more likely to be diagnosed with alcohol or drug disorders. According to the structured diagnostic interview, these sexually aggressive males were also less likely to have social phobia ($p<.025$) and tended to have more Cluster B personality disorder traits (histrionic, narcissistic, borderline, and antisocial). However, the personality disorder differences overall were not significant.

> **17% of sexually aggressive college males meet diagnostic criteria for conduct disorder and substance abuse.**

One study of men from a small Canadian city provides some other interesting findings (Senn, Desmarais, Verberg, & Wood, 2000). Of this random sample of men, 19–83 years of age, 73% reported never being sexually coercive. Regression analysis indicated that childhood abuse, adolescent promiscuity, and restrictive emotionality all significantly increased the likelihood of sexually coercive behavior. The survey used the Sexual Experiences Scale (SES) to assess sexually coercive behavior.

In summary, review of community samples and correctional samples yielded many similar correlates and predictors of sexual violence. Sexual violence was often defined on a continuum of sexual exploitation to child sex abuse, rape, and the most violent, sadistic sexual violence. The influence of childhood abuse, including sexual and physical abuse, was found to be a significant correlate of sexual violence. In addition, poor fathering, along with emotional distancing from the father, were implicated. Behavior control problems in adolescence, adolescent promiscuity, hostility toward women, rape myths, and hyper-masculinity have also been frequently noted precursors of sexually coercive behavior. Alcohol consumption at the time of coercive behavior and as a regular pattern of use has distinguished sexually coercive males from those who are sexually active, but not coercive. Sexual violence occurs in many contexts and most sexual violence does not lead to arrests.

1.5   Course and Prognosis of Sexual Violence

The sexual perpetration careers of both criminal sex offenders and sexually coercive males who have not been arrested have been investigated. Lalumiere et al. (2005) describe a dissertation from Queen's University by W. D. Walker (1997) that examined the careers of rapists. If sexual offenders aggressed against victims less than 16 years of age, male victims, or family victims, then they did tend to specialize in sexual offenses, but those who raped adult women tended to commit other types of crimes. This research also found that if an offender committed two sexual assaults the probability of him committing a third was .50 (and .80 that he would commit another one after his third). The probability of committing another sexual assault steady increased up to .90 that he would assault a seventh victim after six previous assaults. This work on the career trajectory of rapists is important but has not yet been replicated.

Hanson, Morton, and Harris (2003) have reviewed outcome studies and provided some estimates of recidivism for sex offending crimes. The recidivism rates for re-offending range from 10% to 15% after 5 years of living in the community, 20% after 10 years in the community, and 30% to 40% after 20 years. Of course, not all sexual offenses lead to an arrest and so these numbers are probably underestimates. The authors suggest that a more realistic estimate would add 10%–15% to these observed rates. Studies were combined that calculated recidivism rates using re-arrests (5 studies) and convictions (5 studies) of additional sex crimes. These estimates are from both US and Canadian samples and include 4724 released prisoners followed for 20 years.

> **Recidivism rates for sexual offenders 5 years after release from incarceration are 10%–15%, and increase to 20% after 10 years in the community.**

1.5.1   Differences Between Sexually Violent Persons

Not all sex criminals are the same in terms of course and prognosis. Compared to incarcerated individuals with non-sex-related offenses, rapists tend to be very similar to other offenders when adequate controlled comparisons are used. Thus, rapists tend to be generalists in their antisocial behaviors. For example, Bard et al. (1987) examined the clinical files of 100 rapists and found that 93% had committed a previous victimless nonsexual crime and 45% had committed a nonsexual victim crime, like assault, before their index arrest.

There also appear to be important differences between rapists and child molesters. Rice and Harris (1997) compared the histories of 88 rapists with 142 child molesters. Rapists had a more significant history of criminal behavior, including both sexual and nonsexual offenses. They also had higher scores on a measure of psychopathy (PCL-R; Hare, 2003). When released, the rapists were quicker to commit nonsexual offenses, although the child molesters committed sexual offenses sooner.

Of course, not all sex offenders are of equal risk for re-offending. One of the most important research reports in the sex offender literature was conducted by Hanson and Bussiere (1998). This study examined 61 predictive factors of recidivism in a meta-analysis of many studies with a total sample of 28,972 offenders. The study identified 13 factors that predicted that released offenders would commit another sex crime. These factors, along with their correlations with re-offending were, in descending order:

1. Penile plethysmograph (PPG) ratings of deviant sexual interest in children (.32);
2. Clinical assessment of any deviant sexual interest (.22);
3. Prior sex offenses (.19);
4. Treatment dropout (.17);
5. Any stranger victims (.15);
6. Antisocial personality (.14);
7. Any prior offenses (non-sex-related) (.13);
8. Young age of the offender (.13);
9. Early onset of sexual deviance (.12);
10. Being single (never married) (.11);
11. Any related victims (.11);
12. Any boy victims (.11);
13. Diverse sexual crimes (.10).

The top predictors of recidivism include deviant sexual interests, prior sex offenses, being a treatment dropout, any stranger victims, antisocial personality, and boy victims.

Several factors were identified that surprisingly were not helpful in predicting those who would commit future sexual crimes. These included:

1. Victim empathy (.03);
2. Denial of sex offense (.02);
3. Unmotivated for treatment (.01);
4. General psychological problems (.01);
5. Sexually abused as a child (-.01);
6. Degree of sexual contact (-.03).

Hanson et al. (2003) explained that most of the factors that did not predict recidivism were based on judgments made during clinical interviews. Victim empathy and motivation are two examples. We know from research that clinical interviews are not reliable, especially with constructs that are not easily or consistently defined. Thus, because the measures of these concepts most likely are very unreliable, conclusions regarding these factors that did not come out as significant predictors are questionable. However, a variable such as denial by the offender is generally measured by a dichotomous rating and could conceivably be reliably judged. Although denial of the crime would seem to be an important intervention target, the Hanson et al. (2003) research suggests that it is not very predictive of recidivism.

2

Theoretical Models to Explain Sexual Violence

It is important to have a theoretical model that explains sexual violence to rationally guide research, prevention, risk-management, and therapeutic intervention. The most comprehensive model explaining sexual coercive behaviors is that proposed by Knight and Sims-Knight (2003). This work uses Structural Equation Modeling and builds on the work of Malamuth (2003). Malamuth's model is built on the assumption that both criminals and noncriminals manifest similar beliefs, attitudes, and emotions that lead to sexual coercion. This model is referred to as the Hierarchical-Mediational Confluence (HMC) Model.

2.1 Hierarchical-Mediational Confluence Model (HMC)

The model includes personality and behavioral characteristics associated with psychopathic personalities that are predictive of antisocial behavior in general. More proximal risk factors for sexual coercion are personality and behaviors found to be specifically related to sexual aggression including attitudes condoning sexual aggression, dominance for sexual arousal, and heavy pornography consumption. The model proposes that there are two paths to sexual aggression. The first path starts with an abusive home environment (with parental violence or child abuse) that contributes to early delinquent behavior that in turn leads to either general antisocial behavior or impersonal sexuality, including early and promiscuous sexual experiences. Both of these later behavior patterns can lead to sexual aggression if coupled with low empathy and low nurturance. A second path begins with proneness to general hostility (including impulsiveness, irritability, etc.). The general hostility can lead to either general antisocial behavior or acceptance of violence against women, narcissism, hostility to women, and sexual dominance. Either path can lead to sexual aggression if coupled with low empathy or low nurturance. Knight and Sims-Knight (2003) summarize Malamuth's model by describing the two paths of sexual coercion as *sexual promiscuity*, or sociosexuality, and *negative masculinity*, which involves risk-taking, honor defending, and competitive attitudes and behavior.

Malamuth (2003) notes some similarities between the HMC model developed primarily with noncriminals and the psychopathy research that uses primarily criminal populations. Research with both psychopathy and the HMC model has lead to the identification of major predictive factors of sexual violence. Both include early and promiscuous sexual behavior as being important

Helpful theoretical models based on research with community and incarcerated samples can guide treatment.

in later sexual aggression. Also, both have found dominance/power as a source of sexual arousal. Research with psychopathy and with the HMC model indicates that the best prediction occurs when the interaction of different variables is considered rather than just adding their individual influences.

2.2   A Comprehensive Model of Prediction

A weakness in the development of the HMC model, according to Knight and Sims-Knight (2003), is that the testing of the model did not include good measures of developmental antecedents or delinquency. Knight and Sims-Knight (2003) have used the Multidimensional Assessment of Sex and Aggression (Knight, Prentky, & Cerce, 1994) with different populations of criminals, noncriminals, and juveniles to test Malamuth's model. They propose that prediction of violent sexual behavior by three paths better accounts for sexual aggression compared to the two paths in the HMC model. These three paths could be described as:
1. Sexual drive/preoccupation;
2. Antisocial behavior;
3. Callousness/unemotionality.

The major contribution of this modal is the further clarification of early child antecedents of these three paths. In this model, physical /verbal abuse contributes directly to antisocial behavior and to callousness/unemotional responsiveness that indirectly also contributes to antisocial behavior, which then leads to sexual coercion. Sexual abuse in childhood has a separate influence on sexual coercion through sexual fantasies and aggressive sexual fantasies (the sexual drive/preoccupation path). Sexual abuse in childhood becomes more salient as a precursor of sexual preoccupation if certain sexual abuse factors are present in the coercive person's early history. These factors include degree of penetration, amount of coercive force, number of perpetrators, and age of sexual abuse.

The most helpful explanatory models of sexual violence examine the confluence of biology, early childhood experiences, and current environmental influences.

2.3   An Integrated Theory of Sexual Offending

One more comprehensive theory of sexual coercion is important to mention. Ward and Beech (2008) have described their Integrated Theory of Sexual Offending (ITSO). This theory proposes a network of causal factors including biological, ecological, and basic core neuropsychological systems. The biological influences include genetics and evolutionary mechanisms. The ecological niche factors involve social learning influences from cultural and personal circumstances, and the physical environment. Neuropsychological functioning is a third factor that influences motivation and emotions, behavioral controls, action selection, and perception, and memory. Thus, genetics, social learning, and neuropsychological functioning all interact to lead to sexual offending with accompanying, deviant arousal, offense-related thoughts and fantasies, negative or positive emotional states, and social difficulties.

The social learning experiences of the sexually coercive individual are of special interest. Ward and Beech (2008) refers to this component as the ecological niche. The ecological niche of a person is the set of potentially adverse personal circumstances, cultural influences, and physical environments that the person experiences. The psychological system of the person is set by these biological and social learning experiences. Ward and Beech (2008) describe both distal and proximal influences. Once psychological vulnerabilities are acquired, the person will have the propensity not to cope well with environmental stresses. For example, the effects of childhood sexual abuse can lead to psychological disorders and alcohol and substance abuse. In addition, the long-term effects of sexual victimization can include disturbed adult sexual functioning, poor social adjustment, confusion over sexual identity, and inappropriate attempts to reassert masculinity with the potential for abusing others. Also, the experience of war can contribute to the diminution of behavioral controls (Henry, Ward, & Hirshberg, 2004).

Neuropsychological functioning is an important area of research that can help guide our understanding of sexual violence and treatment approaches.

At the heart of this theory is the recognition of the importance of neuropsychological functioning. The neuropsychological functioning of a person has direct influence on motivational/emotional responses, action selection, control systems, and perception and memory. Some of the dynamic variables that have been linked to sexual offending are seen as difficulties of motivation/emotion expression that are controlled by the cortical, limbic, and brainstem structures of the brain. For example, someone brought up in an impoverished environment may have difficulties identifying his emotions and the emotions of others, especially in stressful situations. This may contribute to the development of antisocial or aggressive behavior. This person may also not have developed the social skills necessary to establish strong interpersonal relationships, and as a result may have significant intimacy skills and attachment problems.

Behavioral controls and action selection are associated with the functioning of the frontal cortex, the basal ganglia, and parts of the thalamus. Characteristics seen with sex offenders could be seen as deficits in self-management and self-regulation that are influenced by these brain structures. Some of these deficits include impulsivity, failure to control the expression of negative emotions, not being flexible with adjusting plans based on changing circumstances, and poor problem-solving skills.

Other important areas of perception and memory are influenced by the hippocampal formation and the posterior neocortex. Disturbances in memory and perception can lead to maladaptive cognitions and beliefs and inappropriate interpretation of social interactions. These faulty perceptions and distorted memories can then serve as filters of social information. Some researchers have identified stable dynamic indicators such as cognitive distortions as precursors of sexual offending (Hanson & Harris, 2000; Thornton, 2002).

2.4   A Theory of Interacting Proximal and Distal Predictive Factors

It appears that Ward and Beech's theory (2008) is built on the early theorizing of Marshall and Barbaree (1990). In this modal, sexual abuse of children occurs because of the interacting of proximal and distal factors. Adverse happenings in early childhood have an important influence on later sex offending. These adverse advents include poor parenting, inconsistent and harsh discipline, and physical and sexual abuse. These adverse events lead to distorted internal psychological modals used by the person. These distortions lead to inadequate understanding of relationships, especially with regard to sex and aggression, which in turn leads to poor social and self-management skills very early in life. For these persons, adolescence is an especially important transition time. During this time, they are most receptive to acquiring enduring preferences, interests, and attitudes. The increase in sex hormones at this time supports the establishment and importance of sexually related thinking patterns. Marshall and Barbaree (1990) speculate that the pubertal release of hormones may contribute to the fusing of sex and aggression at this critical age. Ineffective social and self-management skills lead to ineffective attempts at relationships with women that contribute to low self-esteem, anger, and negative attitudes towards women. These intense negative emotions may enhance the potency of sexual desires and even deviant sexual fantasies to achieve what they cannot with their inadequate skills. Compulsive and frequent masturbation can reward mental rehearsal of deviant fantasies. These fantasies, rewarded frequently with masturbation, come to replace important skills of interpersonal closeness, self-esteem, and healthy masculinity.

These vulnerability and more distal factors then interact with more proximal factors and lead to sex offending. Some of these more proximal factors can include stress, intoxication, strong negative affect, sexual stimuli, and the availability of a victim. The sexually coercive behavior in combination with cognitive distortions is thus reinforced in a positive way through sexual arousal and sense of power, and in a negative way through the reduction of low mood.

Adequate theoretical explanations of sexual violence consider the interaction of proximal and distal factors that influence compulsive and psychopathic behaviors.

Clearly, the theory of Ward and Beech (2008) and the earlier theory of Marshall and Barbaree (1990) integrate many factors that can explain the different paths taken to assault victims. These theories are different from those of Malamuth (2003) and Knight and Sims-Knight (2003); for example, they involve a higher level of abstraction and are not based on statistical modeling.

When examined together the modals of sexually offending based on statistical modeling provide important detailed information based on reliable measuring instruments that help define the more general vulnerability factors in the broader theoretical models. For example, the more specific concepts of hostility toward women, the acceptance of rigid masculine roles, and acceptance of aggression are specific concepts that can help us understand the broader concept of anger. Refining these concepts can be helpful in understanding more clearly the schemas of offenders and how to therapeutically address their cognitive distortions. Thus, both the broader and more abstract theories and those based on statistical modeling do contribute to our understanding of sexual coercion.

Hostility toward women, acceptance of rigid masculine roles, and acceptance of aggression are important contributing factors to sexual violence.

2.5   Facilitators of Sexual Violence

As these integrated models indicate, the best explanations for sexually coercive and violent behavior take into consideration the interaction of both distal and proximal factors. There are two proximal factors that have been researched extensively and review of this research is important to better understand the more comprehensive theories. These two proximal factors are the use of pornography and alcohol/drug abuse. Sometimes these proximal factors have been referred to as facilitators of sexual aggression.

2.5.1   Pornography and Sexual Violence

Many years of research and dozens of studies have failed to demonstrate a direct link between the use of pornography and sexual aggression.

Despite many years of research, the evidence for a direct link between the use of pornography and sexual aggression does not exist (Seto, Marc, & Barbaree, 2001). There are three types of studies that address the connection between pornography and sexual coercion. One type of research involves correlation studies of trends at the macro country level. A second type of research examines individual correlations between the use of pornography by those who self-report sexual aggression or actually are arrested for sexual aggression. A third type of research involves laboratory studies that strive for control of extraneous variables and use various dosages of exposure to different kinds of pornography along with proxy measures of sexual aggression. Seto et al. (2001) reviewed the different types of research on the link between pornography and sexual aggression and concluded that those "who are already predisposed to sexually offend are the most likely to show an effect of pornography exposure and are the most likely to show the strongest effects. Men who are not predisposed are unlikely to show an effect" (p. 35).

One of the first steps in any research regarding the effects of pornography on sexual aggression is to operationally define "pornography." The Concise Oxford Dictionary of Current English defines pornography as "the explicit description or exhibition of sexual activity in literature, films, etc., intended to stimulate erotic rather than aesthetic or emotional feelings" (p. 688). Seto et al. (2001) cite the Criminal Code of Canada that provides some important distinctions in types of pornography. The Code refers to three categories of pornography:
1. Explicit sex with violence;
2. Explicit sex without violence but where people are depicted in degrading and humiliating ways;
3. Explicit sex without violence that does not portray people in a degrading or dehumanizing manner.

A distinction is sometimes made between erotica and pornography. Erotica refers to sexually explicit material that portrays adult men and women consensually involved in pleasurable, nonviolent, and nondegrading sexual interactions, whereas pornography has been defined as depictions of sexual activity in which one of the participants is objectified or portrayed as powerless or nonconsenting (Fisher & Barak, 1991). This later definition does not seem to be commonly used, but does distinguish different types of pornography. It appears that it is possible to reliably distinguish violent from nonviolent sexual content in pornography, even though it is questionable that the distinction can be reliably made between sexually explicit stimuli that is degrading or dehumanizing (Seto et al., 2001).

Population level correlation studies are mixed in their results. Some studies indicate that in countries where the use of pornography increases, this increase is not accompanied by an increase in reports of sexual crimes (Kutchinsky, 1991). Another study demonstrated that as the readership of sex magazines increased, the rates of reported rape across several states in the US did increase (Jaffee & Strauss, 1987). The problem with large population correlation studies is that different types of pornography are usually not distinguished and significant confounding factors, such as changes in patterns of arrest rates, cannot be controlled. Therefore, these studies may not be very helpful in clarifying the effects of pornography (Seto et al., 2001).

Individual level data in which the self-reported use of pornography by sex offenders is compared to other comparison groups generally has found no differences. Cook, Fosen, and Pacht (1971) found that sex offenders reported less use of pornography compared to nonsex offenders, and adolescent sex offenders have not reported that pornography played a significant role in their sex offenses (Becker & Stein, 1991). However, there is some evidence that there are differences in use of pornography among different types of sex offenders. For example, child sex offenders use pornography more than rapists (Carter, Prentky, Knight, Vanderveer, & Boucher, 1987). A difficulty with these individual level studies is that factors such as shame may influence the honesty of responses. Also, self-report is not always consistent with actual behavior. For example, research has shown that negative attitudes toward women do not distinguish rapists from nonsex offenders (Marolla & Schully, 1986; Scott & Tetreault, 1987).

Laboratory studies have attempted to assess the causal role of pornography on sexual violence. These studies assess whether exposure to different types and dosages of pornography influence attitudes, beliefs, and cognitions that are associated with sexual coercive behaviors. Typically, paper-and-pencil self-report tests are used to assess these constructs. In other studies, exposure to pornography is related to some analogue of aggression, such as the Buss shock procedure (Donnerstein & Berkowitz, 1981). A great advantage of these experiments is that the type of pornography exposure can be controlled (e.g., violent, degrading, just nudity, etc.). Allen, D'Alessio, and Brezgel (1995) did a meta-analysis of 33 experimental studies on the relationship of pornography and sexual aggression with a total of 2,040 subjects. Results indicated a small increase in nonsexual aggression after exposure to pornography. Depictions of nudity alone decreased subsequent aggressive behavior while violent and nonviolent pornography increased aggressive behavior. Further analysis indicated that only experimental studies that built in a procedure to induce anger in the subjects produced this aggressive behavior after exposure to pornography.

Malamuth and Check (1980) found that prior exposure to violent pornography (e.g., rape) increased arousal at a later exposure to pornography, whereas prior exposure to depictions of consenting sex did not. Marshall, Seidman, and Barbaree (1991) found a similar result. In addition, research has indicated that presenting the female victim of rape as aroused during the forced sexual interaction seems to increase the arousal to the rape scenes. Malamuth and Check (1981) have speculated that this result occurs because it reinforces men who are inclined to be aggressive toward women, believe in rape myths, and have an acceptance of interpersonal violence. Seto (2008) has argued that many of these studies do not take into consideration predisposing factors, such as traits of psychopathy, authoritarianism, hypermasculinity, etc. Malamuth,

Addison, and Koss (2000) reviewed experimental studies and meta-analyses of the effects of pornography on violence and concluded that there is a strong relationship between frequent pornography use and violence for men who are already predisposed to violence. This relationship is especially strong for violent pornography. They suggest that for some men there is a strong connection between sex, power, and aggression, and these men respond differently to pornography than those who do not make these connections in their cognitions and emotionally. These authors utilize research that shows that sexually aggressive men can be primed subliminally with power-related words to make habitual associations between sex and power (Bargh, Raymond, Pryor, & Strack, 1995), whereas normal controls cannot be subliminally primed to make these associations between power and sex. Other research shows that men who make these habitual associations between sex and power are more likely to be sexually aggressive (Zurbriggen, 2000). These are the men who frequently view violent pornography.

This research does not mean that pornography does not have a negative influence on interpersonal relationships. For example, Kenrick, Gutierres, and Goldberg (1989) found that after viewing attractive centerfolds versus abstract art, males expressed being less sexually attracted to their partners and less in love with them. This effect was not found for females. Another study by Zillmann and Bryant (1988) found that both males and females expressed less satisfaction with their partner's appearance, sexual performance, and affection after repeated exposure to pornographic films. Interestingly, Weaver, Masland, and Zillmann (1984) found that males viewing an attractive female nude then rated their partners as less attractive, but males viewing an unattractive female nude rated their partners as more attractive. The authors also added that ratings of attractiveness were not related to satisfaction with the partner.

Thus, even though there are some methodological problems with population level data, individual correlation data and experimental studies, after many years of research, show no significant link between pornography and sexual violence. However, those individuals who may be predisposed to sexual violence may be more likely to seek out violent pornography.

Some experimental evidence even suggests that erotica and nonviolent pornography may reduce proclivity to aggression in men who do not have a predisposition to sexual aggression. However, repeated exposure to pornography under some circumstances may diminish the quality of interpersonal relationships and over time impair the development of good interpersonal skills.

2.5.2　Alcohol Use and Sexual Violence

The second proximal factor that is important in understanding sexual aggression is alcohol consumption. There are three different types of research studies that contribute to our understanding of the link between alcohol intake and sexual aggression. These are: (1) Correlation studies of alcohol consumption and history of sexual aggression; (2) Studies that examine the contribution of consumption of alcohol at the time of the sexual aggression; and (3) Experimental studies that directly test the causal connection between alcohol consumption and sexual aggression.

Some studies have shown high rates of alcoholism among rapists (e.g., 35%, Rada, 1978). Others have argued that nonviolent and violent nonsex offenders are just as likely as rapists to abuse alcohol (Langevin & Lang, 1990). Nonincarcerated males who self-report sexually coercive behavior are more likely to report current use of alcohol and drugs (Borowsky, Hogan, & Ireland, 1997), even when background factors such as child abuse, gang membership, and emotional health are controlled. Others have found that those who self-report sexually coercive behavior and meet the diagnosis for alcohol abuse or dependence (53%) also show symptoms of conduct disorder, personality disorders or other signs of psychopathology (Quimette, 1997). As can be seen from these few studies, the relationship between alcohol and sexual violence is complex and not as simple as commonly assumed.

More sophisticated causal modeling studies have demonstrated there is a relationship between alcohol consumption and self-reported sexual coercion, but this relationship is not direct and is mediated by other factors. Abbey, McAuslan and Ross (1998) found that sex-related alcohol expectancies and sexual experiences predicted alcohol consumption, and alcohol consumption predicted self-reported sexual coercion. However, these relationships were found to be indirect through the misperception of victim sexual intent and the likelihood of being unpunished if sexual assault took place.

Summary analyses of this literature indicates that correlation studies do show a relationship between alcohol use and sexual violence, but a good part of this relationship can be explained by the presence of other factors, such as psychopathology and distorted perceptions of victim responsibility, and likelihood of not being punished following the sexual assault (Testa, 2002). Many of these correlation studies do not distinguish very well the nature of the assaultive behavior nor whether alcohol was consumed at the time of the assault and therefore little can be concluded about the direct impact of alcohol consumption on sexual aggression (Testa, 2002).

A second way of examining the link between alcohol use and sexual aggression examines the consumption of alcohol at the actual time of the sexual aggression. Past reviews of alcohol use by rapists at the time of the sexual violence range from 13% to 63% (Roizen, 1997) and 3% to 72% among juvenile sex offenders (Lightfoot & Barbaree, 1993). There is wide variation in incidence of alcohol use at the time of sexual violence reported by authorities from different jurisdictions, ranging from 77% in Chicago to 37% in Massachusetts (Ullman, Karabatsos, & Koss, 1999). There are some dramatic differences in alcohol use across different sex crimes with rapists and other violent criminals having rates of 75% and 90%, respectively, versus 13% for child molesters (Gudjonsson & Sigurdsson, 2000). In contrast to this variability of data from perpetrators of sex crimes, 60–65% of community and college samples consistently report use of alcohol or drugs at the time of the sexually coercive behavior (Testa, 2002).

However, these rates of occurrence of alcohol consumption and sexual violence may not mean that alcohol consumption directly contributes to sexual aggression, since alcohol consumption is also present in nonsexual violence, with consensual sex, and in social settings such as bars. One unique study of college students tried to address this problem of confounding variables by looking at the same individuals who reported on both sexually aggressive

Correlation studies show a relationship between sexual violence and alcohol use, but a good part of this relationship is explained by psychopathology and distorted perceptions of victim responsibility, and likelihood of being punished.

dates and dates where sexual aggression did not occur (Muehlenhard & Linton, 1987). Although alcohol or drugs were involved in both sexually aggressive and nonaggressive dates (60%), heavy drinking of both the perpetrator and victim was more prevalent in the sexually aggressive dates.

It could be expected that the presence of alcohol at the time of the sexual assault would increase the severity of the aggression and the possibility of injury. Testa (2002) has reviewed the literature and found inconsistent findings regarding whether offender drinking was related to the severity of the sexual assault, such as completed versus attempted rape, and physical injury. For example, Brecklin and Ullman (2002) used data from the National Violence Against Women Survey (NVAWS) and found that completed rape (versus attempted rape) was almost twice as likely when offenders were drinking heavily. This study also controlled for victim characteristics and drinking. However, Ullman et al. (1999) found with a sample of 694 men that substance abuse at the time of the assault did not predict sexual aggression severity. Instead, the study found that other variables more directly influenced degree of aggression at the time of the assault. These variables included victim alcohol use at the time of the assault, victim resistance, and frequency of intoxication of the offender.

Because of problems with operational definitions of alcohol consumption and sexual assault, along with difficulties with adequacy of measures, the causal connection between alcohol consumption and sexual aggression remains unclear (Testa, 2002). Research studies often rate alcohol consumption and severity of sexual aggression in a dichotomous manner. Dichotomous measures (e.g., consumes alcohol or does not consume alcohol) can often result in unreliable measurements because of the complexity of the variable being measured. In an effort to assess the relationship between sexual assault and alcohol consumption, Abbey, Clinton, McAuslan, Zawacki, and Buck (2002) used continuous measures of these variables. It is often assumed that there is a linear relationship between alcohol consumption and sexual aggression, with increasing levels of alcohol intake being associated with increasing levels of severity of sexual assault. You could also predict that there is a curvilinear relationship, because at very high levels of intoxication the perpetrator may pass out or not be able to achieve or sustain an erection. Surprisingly, the study found an unexpected curvilinear relationship. Injuries were greatest in assaults committed by sober offenders or those who were highly intoxicated. Also consistent with other studies, victim injury was associated with the victim being intoxicated. In fact, victim intoxication was a stronger predictor of sexual assault outcomes than perpetrator alcohol use.

In contrast to the above correlation studies, the conclusions from experimental research on the proximal effects of alcohol consumption are much less murky. Experimental research has consistently found both a direct pharmacological effect of alcohol on acceptance of sexual aggression and an indirect path of acceptance of sexual aggression through the mediating variable of expectancy (Testa, 2002). There are two cautionary concerns with this research. First, most of this research has been done with subjects that have not been arrested for their sexual assaults, and these results may not generalize to criminal populations. Second, the outcome measures of most of this research are self-reported acceptance of sexual assault under different manipulated conditions. The question of whether self-report of acceptance of sexual assault translates into sexually assaultive behavior is uncertain.

A useful theory of explaining these experimental studies is alcohol myopia (Steel & Josephs, 1990). This theory maintains that sexual aggression is caused by a pharmacological impairment of the ability to accurately discern inhibitory cues. Johnson, Noel, and Sutter (2000) provide some confirmation of the myopia effect of alcohol intake on sexual aggression. Subjects in an experiment were placed in four separate conditions of no alcohol, placebo, low dose of alcohol (BAL .02), or moderate dose (BAL .065). They were then shown a video of a date rape situation in which the woman showed some sexual interest or in which the woman was clearly sexually unreceptive. As expected, there was a clear relationship between alcohol dosage and whether forced sex with each date partner was judged to be acceptable. In the high alcohol dosage condition, the woman's unreceptiveness did not inhibit the judged acceptability of forced sex. However, Testa (2002) cautions that the myopia explanation may not be adequate and leaves out research findings that other factors such as expectancies and sexual arousal are significant mediators of alcohol ingestion and sexual violence. For example, men who consume alcohol and who are high in hypermasculinity are more callous toward depictions of victims of sexual assault in laboratory analogue situations compared to men low in hypermasculinity and who consume alcohol. The latter group is actually more empathic and show high inhibitions against sexual aggression (Norris, George, Davis, Martell, & Leonesio, 1999). Thus, there appears to be direct pharmacological alcohol effects on sexual violence. Alcohol expectancies also influence sexual aggression, both independently and in interaction with the pharmacological alcohol effects.

One mediating variable that has not been researched extensively is that of sexual arousal. However, alcohol expectancies have been found to predict self-reported sexual arousal and perceived interest in another person (George, Stoner, Norris, Lopez, & Lehman, 2000). These researchers also found evidence that when the expectation of alcohol is coupled with actual ingestion instead of a placebo, sexual excitement to sexually explicit stimuli is increased.

Testa (2001) suggests an overall theoretical model that takes into consideration a number of proximal and distal variables that effect how alcohol consumption influences the perpetration of sexual violence. Individual differences, such as alcohol expectancies, hypermasculinity, attitudes toward violence, prior sexual activity, impulsivity, and antisocial behavior have direct causal effects on sexual aggression, but also interact with the separate pharmacological effects of alcohol consumption. In addition, these individual differences influence the selection of the context in which alcohol is consumed (e.g., bar, college party, etc.) and interpretation of what behaviors are expected of abusers and victims. For example, some have argued that bar attendance is related to physical and sexual violence independent of the effects of alcohol (Parks & Miller, 1997).

It is helpful to review one final controlled laboratory experiment that examines the causal connection between sexual aggression and alcohol, sexual arousal, and violent pornography (Davis, Norris, George, Martell, & Heiman, 2006). A sample of 84 social drinkers from the community was assigned to the alcohol condition (i.e., provided alcohol until a .07 BAL was achieved) or

Research suggests a pharmacological effect of alcohol on sexual violence, but this effect interacts with alcohol expectancies, hypermasculinity, prior sexual activity, attitudes toward violence, impulsivity, and antisocial behavior.

no alcohol condition. A stimulus story was presented in which a female and male in a social situation were said to have consumed three to four glasses of wine. The male makes sexual advances to the female who initially resists verbally and physically. After the first explicitly described sex act, the female is described as either experiencing pleasure or distress. Subjects were given a self-report scale of sexual arousal. In addition, the subjects were asked if they themselves would have acted as the male character in the story under the same circumstances. The results indicate that self-reported sexual arousal was significantly related to the likelihood that the subject would commit sexual violence. Surprisingly, alcohol intoxication was not directly related to men's self-reported likelihood of sexual aggression. However, intoxication did lead to self-reported sexual arousal to violent sexual stimuli, which in turn predicted self-reported likelihood of rape. Also, alcohol-related beliefs did directly increase sexual arousal for some men. That is, those men who believed that alcohol increased women's vulnerability to rape experienced greater sexual arousal, regardless of whether they were intoxicated or not. This may indicate acceptance of the belief that an aggressive sexual advance towards a women who is consuming alcohol is justified. This would be in line with research showing that drinking rape victims are judged more harshly than nondrinking partners (Richardson & Campbell, 1982). For some men, the thought of sexual dominance or power over a vulnerable woman may be arousing. This includes women who are intoxicated. Also, men were more sexually aroused when the victim indicated some pleasure after the attack. These subjects were perhaps aroused because they believed that not only was sexually violent behavior tolerated, but it was desired. Surprisingly, this rape supportive effect and arousal was present whether the subjects were intoxicated or sober.

This summary of findings regarding the effects of pornography and alcohol on sexual aggression has a number of implications for intervention and treatment. The strong influence of alcohol abuse and/or dependence, and alcohol consumption at the time of sexual violence cannot be underestimated. It is clear that there are direct pharmacological effects of alcohol use on sexual violence, and therefore alcohol treatment must be an important component of effective treatment programs. However, the influence of individual differences, such as hypermasculinity, antisocial behavior, hostility toward women, and acceptance of violence interact with the direct effects of alcohol to lead to sexual violence. Therefore, these individual factors must also be addressed in treatment. Clearly, alcohol intoxication and expectancies can be used as a way for sexually violent individuals to escape responsibility for their actions and negatively influence empathy, hostility, and antisocial attitudes. Also, the attribution of cause to pornography for violent behavior is not justified by the research, despite popular media portrayals of pornography being a significant factor in dramatic serial killings like those of Ted Bundy. It does appear that violent pornography does enhance aggression when violence is directly modeled and rewarded and rape myths are supported. Thus, healthy intimacy, sexual fulfillment, and healthy adult attachment strategies should be a focus of treatment. Research on the effects of alcohol and pornography on sexual violence shows that there is a tendency for some men to become sexually aroused when the vulnerability of potential victims is portrayed. This finding

Research findings on facilitators of sexual violence suggests the need for treatment to focus on healthy intimacy and adult attachment strategies.

may underscore the need to address dominance and control motives in men who are sexually violent.

2.6 The Influence of Early Childhood Abuse and/or Neglect

In addition to these two important proximal factors, a distal factor that may significantly influence the likelihood of sexual aggression is an early history of childhood neglect and abuse, and sexual abuse in particular. A recent meta-analysis examined 17 studies with comparisons between 1,037 sexual offenders and 1,762 nonsexual offenders (Jespersen, Lalumiere, & Seto, 2009). The authors found a significant relationship between sexual abuse as a child and later sexual offending against others. Groups of sexual offenders versus nonsexual offenders did not differ in terms of physical abuse history. Interestingly, further analysis showed that early sexual abuse of the offender predicted sexual abuse of children but not of adults.

2.7 Prevention

In light of the recognized problem of sexual violence on college campuses, the federal government has made rape prevention programs a requirement for colleges receiving federal aid (Heppner, Good, Hillenbrand-Gunn, & Hawkins, 1995). However, the effectiveness of these programs at actually reducing rape has yet to be demonstrated. Some of the problems with the evaluation of the effectiveness of rape prevention problems include a lack of research with rigorous designs, lack of a behavioral outcome, such as actual reduction of coercive behavior, and some confusion over the psychological targets of the prevention efforts.

The effectiveness of prevention programs at actually reducing rape has yet to be demonstrated.

A number of key factors have been linked to coercive sexual behaviors in the literature of sexual violence on college campuses. These include rape myth acceptance, sex role stereotyping, adversarial sexual beliefs, acceptance of interpersonal violence, sexual conservatism, attitudes toward women, and low levels of empathy toward victims. Different scales have been developed to measure these variables. Sample measures of these variables are then correlated with self-reported sexual arousal to scenarios of sexual coercion or change in attitudes in one or more of these measures.

The content of sexual violence prevention programs varies considerable. In one meta-analysis of 45 evaluations of rape prevention programs with 153 comparisons, 50% of the programs were between 30 and 60 minutes in duration, 33% were over 60 minutes in duration, and 9.6% involved a full college course (Brecklin & Forde, 2001). The outcome variable in this meta-analysis was limited to rape-supportive attitude change. The overall result was positive with an effect size of .35, with 82% of the comparisons showing positive attitude change. In 37.9% of the programs, the posttests were given immediately after the program with the follow-up varying from 1 to 10 weeks for the other comparisons. Further analysis in this study indicated that males in mixed groups of women and men did not do as well as in all male groups. Unfortunately, positive attitude change decreased with longer follow-up times.

The selection of the specific targets of intervention is important in rape prevention programs. Schewe and O'Donohue (1993, 1996) demonstrated that prevention efforts that emphasize victim empathy rather than modifying rape myths were more effective in reducing self-reported likelihood of committing sexual abuse. In fact, these authors argue that a fact-oriented approach to dispelling rape myths has little effect on high-risk subjects compared to the victim empathy approach. In fact, high-risk males may learn in didactic groups that rape is a low-risk behavior since so few rapes are reported. It is also possible that facts alone are not enough to produce a change in rape potential. In the victim empathy experimental condition, a 45-minute video was presented with several victims of rape including child sexual abuse and sexual harassment victims telling about their abuse and their resulting suffering. Subjects were told during the video to imagine how a woman would feel before, during, and after being sexually assaulted, harassed, or abused as a child. They also were guided through scenarios and were told to image themselves as the victims. The primary focus was the cognitive and emotional aspects of being victimized. A second tape of 45 minutes presented facts about rape, sexual harassment, and child sex abuse. The purpose was to dispel rape myths. The content was patterned after programs that had been previously judged as being successful at dispelling rape myths. This study is instructive at emphasizing that emotional reactance and increase in victim empathy seems to be important targets for successful prevention efforts with high-risk men.

Lonsway (1996) reviewed 20 years of research on rape prevention programs. Unfortunately, most measures of effectiveness were found to be inadequate. Most studies measured either attitude change immediately after presentation of the prevention program or simply asked if participants liked the program. Missing were any measures of persistence of attitude change or actual behavioral changes in follow-up. Out of 15 co-educational programs, six found no change in men's attitudes, four showed immediate change only, and two limited their outcome measures to satisfaction. Two others were semester long courses that produced little change in attitude – in fact, one actually made men worse. Out of the seven all-male programs reviewed, four were successful in showing immediate attitude change without any measures of persistency of these attitude changes, two limited their outcomes to satisfaction ratings, and one made men worse. After this review, the author made the following recommendations for effective rape-prevention programs: Allow time for interactive participation, discuss gender roles and the status of women, increase empathy for rape victims, use an approach that confronts ideology, not the person, use all-male environments, and use peer educators.

An example of a rape prevention program built on the above effectiveness principles is The Men's Program (Foubert, 2005). The program is designed to challenge rape myths, values that involve hostility to women, and masculine stereotypes that indirectly contribute to abuse, violence, and rape. The program, which involves only men, is designed to help participants understand how to help women recover from a rape experience. The core of the program is a peer-education and victim empathy approach. A video of the rape of a male

Even though the research is weak, all-male, peer-guided, and a victim empathy focus seem to all be important in effective sexual violence prevention programs.

police officer is used to dramatize for the participants the feelings of helplessness, fear, humiliation of the hospital visit, and concern about sexually transmitted disease. In a seven-month follow-up of the Men's Program, 195 college males from eight fraternities were assessed on rape myth acceptance scores with a standard scale and on likelihood of raping scores with a standard scale. The rape myth acceptance scores significantly decreased after the program, but these changes did not persist at seven-month follow-up. The likelihood of raping scores showed significant improvement both after the program and seven months later (Foubert, 2000).

These prevention efforts are encouraging, but the supportive research is weak. It appears that an all-male, peer-guided, and victim empathy focus is important. The potential cost savings in terms of human suffering and dollars for incarceration and treatment should compel us to devote more resources to good outcome research and implementation efforts for those programs that we know work. Even though these prevention programs have been primarily at the college age students, we know that attitudes regarding macho masculine stereotypes, acceptance of violence, and hostility toward women are present in early adolescence. Therefore, efforts at prevention of sexual violence in high schools and in community settings are needed.

3

Diagnosis

3.1   Differential Diagnosis

The currently accepted system for diagnosing individuals with sexual violence problems is the DSM IV-TR (American Psychiatric Association, 2000). Most sexually violent individuals are diagnosed as having a paraphilia and an impulse control disorder. There are four basic criteria associated with the DSMIV-TR diagnoses of paraphilia: (1) "Recurrent, intense sexually arousing fantasies, sexual urges, or behaviors"; (2) "Generally involving nonhuman objects, the suffering or humiliation of oneself or one's partner, or children, or other nonconsenting persons"; (3) Has occurred "over a period of at least 6 months"; and (4) "The behavior, sexual urges, or fantasies cause clinically significant distress or impairment in social, occupational, or other important areas of functioning" (p. 566).

A number of writers have pointed out diagnostic problems with the DSM IV-TR description of paraphilia when applied to sexually violent men (Doren, 2002; Marshall, 2006b). The literature on child sexual abuse is confusing because some people use the term "pedophile" to refer to all child molesters even if they do not meet the criteria for the DSM IV-TR diagnosis of paraphilia. Some authors distinguish between pedophiles who molest prepubescent children and those who molest postpubescent children (referred to as hebephiles). Also, there is no specific category for men who are repeat rapists, so clinicians tend to use the category of paraphilia, NOS (not otherwise specified). There are no specific guidelines for diagnosing rape as a paraphilia, NOS.

There is no specific paraphilia diagnosis for repeat rapists.

3.1.1   Unreliability of Paraphilia Diagnoses

Any valid diagnostic system should be supported with research on reliability. A commonly accepted type of reliability is inter-rater reliability. This reliability check is accomplished by having different clinicians use the system with the same clients to determine if they arrive at the same diagnosis. Unfortunately, reliability research has not supported the DSM IV-TR category of paraphilia. Marshall (2006b) emphasized that the statistical literature indicates that for important decisions, reliability estimates ought to be at least .9, using the kappa statistic to calculate reliability. The DSM field trials resulted in a kappa of .92 for a combined group of psychosexual disorders and paraphilias. However, combining these two groups does not make sense because very different presenting problems are being diagnosed, and the diagnostic criteria for each group are very different. Nevertheless, even with this combined group, there were only 7 cases in the test sample and this is clearly inadequate for research purposes. In a second field trial, another 5 cases were diagnosed by clinicians, but then the kappa fell to .75 (O'Donohue, Regev, & Hagstrom, 2000). Even though these reliability checks were inadequate, paraphilia remains a diagnostic category in DSM IV-TR.

Fortunately, a robust DSM reliability study on paraphilia was conducted on a sample of all sexual violent predators evaluated in the state of Florida from June 2000 through June 2001 (Levenson, 2004). The diagnostic reliability was assessed with four specific paraphilia categories and with two different clinicians applying DSM criteria to 295 inmates. The resultant kappa reliabilities were as follows: pedophilia (.65), sexual sadism (.30), exhibitionism (.47), and for paraphilia, NOS (.36). The reliability for the presence of any paraphilia was unacceptably low (.47).

The diagnostic categories of paraphilia have not achieved acceptable levels of reliability.

3.1.2   Problems with DSM IV-TR Criteria of Paraphilia

Other issues arise with the criteria for the paraphilias. For example, the diagnostic manual of the American Psychiatric Association reads "isolated sexual acts with children do not warrant the diagnosis of pedophila" (p. 271, DSM IV-TR). It is unclear what this means. Perhaps someone has been very stressed and has been having sexual fantasies about children and acknowledges one episode of genital contact with a child. Would the diagnosis of paraphilia apply in this case? Also, the category of pedophilia only applies to child molesters who have "recurrent intense sexual urges and sexually arousing fantasies involving sexual activity with a prepubescent child or children." For example, a person who becomes a bus driver to stimulate fantasies, but never acts on these fantasies, could conceivably be diagnosed as a person with a paraphilia. Criteria B of DSM IV-TR also has the requirement that "the person has acted on these urges, or the sexual urges or fantasies cause marked distress or interpersonal difficulties" (p. 572). Marshall (2006b) contends that most clinicians believe that the presence of deviant fantasies and urges is a necessary requirement for a diagnosis of paraphilia, according to DSM IV-TR. But, many men who molest children are given this diagnosis, even though there is little evidence to verify the presence of deviant sexual fantasies (Fist & Halon, 2008).

The word "intense" is also problematic in the criteria for paraphilia. Marshall (1997a) found that 60% of nonfamilial offenders and 75% of incest offenders report having recurrent fantasies or urges, but these fantasies were reported to be transitory and tended to occur immediately before the offense. Does "intense" mean more persistent than other fantasies, or more vivid, or something else?

There are four ways that clinicians and researchers have tried to measure these urges and fantasies, and the reliability of each of these methods has been called into question (Looman & Marshall, 2005; Seto, 2008). The four methods are: (1) Self-report; (2) Psychometric testing; (3) Phallometric testing; and (4) Attention timing to images.

3.1.3   Significant Problems with the Diagnosis of Sadism

It would seem that the most violent sexual patterns of behavior should be most reliably categorized with a diagnosis, if the diagnostic system has utility. However, the diagnosis for sadism is most questionable in light of the finding of Levenson (2004) documenting very low reliability (kappa of only .30). The DSM IV-TR criteria for sadism read: "Recurrent, intense, sexually arousing fantasies, sexual urges, or behaviors involving acts (real, not simulated) in which the psychological or physical suffering (including humiliation) of the victim is sexually exciting to the person" (p. 574). Marshall, Kennedy, and Yates (2002) examined 10 years of records of offenders diagnosed as sadists in Canadian prisons and compared these sadists to nonsadist sex offenders. Remarkably, those categorized as nonsadists were more likely to beat or torture their victims, their crimes had more generally accepted sadistic features, and they were more aroused by nonsexual violence on phallometric testing. However, sadists were more aroused by normal consenting sex. The results of this study are totally opposite what would be expected and replication is needed. A follow-up study by these same researchers attempted to introduce more experimental control than possible with a broad record review. Marshall, Kennedy, Yates, and Serran (2002) asked 15 psychiatrists to diagnose 12 sexual offenders and provided four packages of systematically collected information to use in the diagnostic process. The packages of information included detailed social histories, phallometric testing results, psychological reports, and offense history. Interdiagnostic reliability among the 15 psychiatrists was very low (kappa=.14). These two studies were from the same group of researchers, and thus could be challenged. However, other descriptive studies of sadists have been very inconsistent and add further to the questionable meaning of the sadism diagnosis.

> **The reliability and thus validity of the diagnosis of sadism is highly questionable.**

There have been several descriptive studies of sadists with conflicting definitions, varying sample characteristics and inconsistent results. For example, Dietz, Hazelwood, and Warren (1990) provided data on 34 sex offenders described as sadists. Twenty of these offenders had also killed their victims, with 17 being described as serial murderers. Of the 34, 50% had significant histories of alcohol/drug abuse, 35% had prior violent offenses, and 80% had reported sadistic sexual fantasies, with 20–45% also reporting other paraphilia traits. This study described sadists as outwardly good citizens with 30% being involved in charity events, 50% married, and 75% being employed at the time of their offense. These results stand in marked contrast with those of a prior study by Brittain (1970), who described a sample of sadists as socially withdrawn, shy, and introverted.

Dietz et al. (1990) also found that 93.3% of sadistic acts were planned. All of the victims were tortured and 87% were tied up and gagged. In 73% of the cases, sodomy was committed, with 57% involving sexual intercourse, and 71% fellatio. The victim was unknown to the victim in 83% of the cases. These different results can be partially attributed to sampling bias, but it is difficult for scientists to have any confidence in the diagnosis of sadism.

MacCulloch, Snowden, Wood, and Mills (1983) collected data on a small sample of sadists and reported that these men started experiencing interpersonal problems during adolescence, which contributed to social isolation and low self-esteem. Of the men studied, 79% reported deviant sexual fantasies that became increasingly violent and 54% reported "tryouts," such as breaking into a woman's apartment and watching her sleep. Langevin et al. (1985) compared 9 sadists, 11 nonsadist sex offenders, and 20 nonsexual and nonviolent offenders. The sadists reported feelings of sexual inadequacy (63%), a low sexual desire (38%), fear of becoming a homosexual (38%), anger towards women (38%), and difficulty talking to women (75%). As children, they reported being punished for temper tantrums and enuresis. None of the sadists showed a psychopathic profile on the MMPI, but they did report a history of cerebral difficulties, frontal lobe impairment, and nonspecific neurological problems. Gratzer and Bradford (1995) compared 28 sadists (20 serial murderers and 8 sexual aggressors) and 29 nonsadists (14 serial murderers and 15 sexual aggressors). Sadists reported a pattern of deviant behaviors before their crimes including transvestitism, voyeurism, and exhibitionism. They also reported being detached during the assault (82.1%) and using severe coercive means such as torture (78.6%) and blows resulting in injuries (64.3%). The study also found that 86% met criteria of a diagnosis of antisocial personality and reported neurological difficulties and 50% reported a sexual dysfunction. Clearly, these descriptive studies do not present a consistent picture of this unreliable diagnosis. The discrepancies among these studies can be attributed to use of selective samples and variations in how descriptive data were collected and measured.

One study on sadism was conducted with methodological rigor and superior sample selection and assessment. Proulx, Blais, and Beauregard (2006) screened 95% of all sex offenders evaluated at a Regional Reception Center of Correctional Services in Canada from 1995 through 2000. They used phallometric rating of responses to violence, and two specific sadism scales to finalize a "true" sample of 43 sadist subjects, including 18 sexual murderers and 25 sexual aggressors. This group was then compared to a matched sample of nonsadist sexual aggressors.

The results of this study do present a picture of sadism based on rigorous methodology rather than convenience samples and interview data that are problematic in other descriptive research on sadism. This well-designed study documented that both sadists and nonsadists were exposed to violence as children (51.2% versus 42.3%), physically abused (55.8% versus 44.3%), with many having been abandoned as children (51.2% versus 39.2%). More sadists than nonsadists were exposed to psychological violence (e.g., humiliation) (62.8% versus 43.3%). Before the age of 18, sadists tended to be more deviant in their behaviors, and experienced more social isolation (52.5% versus 34.7%), and temper tantrums (47.5% versus 25.5%). Their early deviance was very sexual in nature with more sadists than nonsadists using pornographic videos (35.7% versus 18.1%), visiting strip clubs (31% versus 10.5%), engaging in compulsive masturbation (25% versus 11.7%), and experiencing deviant sexual fantasies (48.8% versus 18.6%).

There is agreement among researchers that most sadists use bondage along with psychological and physical torture.

Both sadist and nonsadist sex offenders tended to be generalists in their crimes with only approximately 40% of their offenses being sexual. During phallometric testing, sadists tended to be more responsive when humiliation and physical violence were inlcuded as a part of the rape scenes. They did not differ on phallometric testing to nonsexual violence. This later finding would support the idea that sex and violence become fused for these individuals.

Psychological testing in this study was very instructive. On the Millon Clinical Multiaxial Inventory (MCMI), sadists had significantly higher scores on avoidant, schizoid, and schizotypal scales compared to nonsadists. It was found that 58.3% were characterized as having a profile described as avoidant, schizoid, and dependent with passive-aggressive features. In contrast, 62% of nonsadist sexual aggressors had prominent narcissistic and antisocial characteristics. These results do not comport with the assumption that sadist sexual offenders have psychopathic personalities.

> **Sadists tend to have avoidant, schizoid, or schizotypal personality traits.**

Within 48 hours of the crime, the sadists expressed more anger in general and specific anger toward women (58.5% versus 21.1%). The sadists reported that anger was the primary emotion at the time of crime (65.8% versus 39%), even though deviant sexual fantasies were also reported (46.5% versus 17.3%). There were no differences on diversity of sexual activity (e.g., intercourse, fellatio, cunnilingus, and sodomy). In general, sadists planned their offense in more detail, selected their victim, kidnapped and confined the victim, used bondage, a weapon, psychological torture, physical torture and mutilation, specific mutilation of the erogenous zones, inserted objects into the vagina, and were more likely to kill their victims (37.2% versus 22.4%). Most significant are the findings that only sadists used bondage, physical torture, mutilation of the erogenous zones, and insertion of objects into the vagina. Sadists were more likely to use asphyxiation (50% versus 27.3%), leave the body completely naked (88.2% versus 11.8%), engage in postmortem intercourse (31.3% versus 0%), and engage in postmortem mutilation (44.4% versus 0%). In contrast to this research, Hazelwood, Dietz, and Warren (1992) have argued that postmortem mutilations do not characterize sadists because they need a live victim who can experience suffering and humiliation, and therefore the postmortem mutilations actually represent attempts to make it difficult to identify the victim's remains. Again, the contrast in research findings with other less controlled studies is instructive. Only sadists engage in postmortem mutilation and postmortem intercourse. Perhaps having sex with a dead victim is perceived as total control.

The current state of research calls into question the reliability, and therefore the usefulness, of the diagnosis of paraphilia. There continues to be significant confusion over specific categories of paraphilia, such as pedophilia. The most questionable diagnostic category is that of sadism. The poor reliability of the diagnosis of sadism is illustrated by the inconsistency of the descriptive studies of this most violent type of sexual aggression.

3.2   Co-Morbidity and Co-Occurring Diagnoses

> **60–70% of paraphilic males have a diagnosis of dysthymic disorder.**

There are a growing number of studies showing that many sexual offenders who are incarcerated and noncriminal offenders in community samples meet criteria for Axis I, DSM IV-TR diagnoses other than paraphilia. For example, 60–70% of paraphilic males also have a diagnosis of dysthymic disorder (Kafka & Hennon, 2002). In one study of pedophiles, it was found that 56% also reported a lifetime diagnosis of major depression (Raymond, Coleman, Ohlerking, Christenson, & Miner, 1999). There is also a high prevalence of bipolar disorder (35–55%) among sex offenders (Dunsieth, Nelson, Brusman-Lovins et al., 2004). In general, symptoms reflective of anxiety and mood disorders are more frequently reported by incarcerated sexual offenders than nonsexual offenders (Almeyer, Kleinsasser, Stoner, & Retzlaff, 2003). Social phobia has also been reported as prevalent in paraphilic males (20–30%) and in convicted sex offenders (Dunsieth et. al, 2004; Kafka & Hennon, 2002). Hoyer, Kunst, and Schmidt (2001) reported a lifetime prevalence rate of 53% of social phobia for paraphilic sexual offenders compared to 20% for mentally disordered nonsexual offenders. Accompanying this high prevalence of social phobia are associated social skills deficits (Almeyer et al., 2003).

> **53% of sex offenders report a lifetime prevalence of social phobia.**

The research on co-morbidity of alcohol abuse and sexual violence is inconsistent, primarily as a result of differences in how researchers assess the level of alcohol abuse (Kafka, 2008). In one study that utilized rigorous methodology, the lifetime rates of psychoactive substance abuse, including alcohol abuse, were found to be 82% for paraphilic males and 100% for nonparaphilic sexual offenders in a sample of 113 (Dunsieth et al., 2004). In other reports, 28–50% of sexual offenders were diagnosed with current alcohol abuse or dependence (Kafka, 2008).

> **Common co-morbid diagnoses include substance abuse, antisocial personality disorder, ADHD, PTSD, Tourette syndrome, Asperger syndrome, and head injuries.**

A common belief is that adult Attention Deficit Hyperactivity Disorder (ADHD) is a frequent co-condition of sexual offending. In fact, ADHD is becoming more recognized as a significant co-morbid diagnosis for adolescents who are sexually aggressive. One study reported a co-morbidity rate of 77% for 35 children/adolescents that were being evaluated for sexually aggressive behavior (Fago, 1999). Another study reported a rate of 71% for adolescents who sexually molested other children (Galli et al., 1999). The retrospective determination of ADHD in sexually aggressive adult males is difficult because of the unreliability of self-report used to make this diagnosis. Kafka and Hennon (2002) reported a rate of 36–53% for self-reported symptoms meeting criteria for ADHD in sex offenders; this rate was significantly higher than in offenders of nonsexual crimes.

Other disorders that have been identified as possible co-morbid disorders include fetal alcohol spectrum disorders, Tourette syndrome, autism spectrum disorders (especially Asperger syndrome), mental retardation, schizophrenias, head injuries, and neurogenerative disorders (Kafka, 2008). Clearly these disorders are related to impulse control and suggest that sex offending can be viewed as an impulse control or compulsive disorder.

The prevalence of posttraumatic stress disorder (PTSD) among sexually violent men is not clear. It is true that sexually violent men experience significant emotional, sexual, and physical abuse. There does seem to be a specific relationship between sexual abuse and later committing a sexual offense against children (Jespersen et al., 2009). Macpherson (2003) has reported lower rates of developmental adversity, including physical and sexual abuse, among hands-off sex offenders (e.g., exhibitionism) versus hands-on sexual offenders (e.g., rape). However, this relationship would be complicated by predisposing factors to PTSD and the co-occurrence of factors such as unstable caretaker behavior.

Antisocial Personality Disorder (ASP) is often found to be the most frequent Axis II diagnosis among sex offenders (Levenson, 2004). However, clinically, it is important to consider that a significant subpopulation of sexually aggressive individuals with ASP also experienced other co-morbid disorders that may have contributed to a pattern of aggressive and asocial behaviors. Some of these disorders include ADHD, substance abuse, conduct disorder, and PTSD. Even psychopathy, which is not a diagnosis but a clinically determined construct, may have been influenced in childhood and early adolescence by other co-morbid conditions, such as ADHD, bipolar disorder, Asperger syndrome, and conduct disorder (Kafka, 2008; Piatogorsky & Hinshaw, 2004). Other Axis II diagnoses sometimes seen in sexually aggressive males include avoidant personality, narcissistic personality, and schizoid personality.

3.3   Sexual Coercion and Hypersexuality

Another important biological predisposition that may contribute to sexual coercive behavior is high sexual appetite or hypersexuality (Kafka, 2008). According to DSMIV-TR criteria, by definition, paraphilic individuals are characterized by "recurrent, intense sexually arousing urges or behaviors" (American Psychiatric Association, 2000, p. 566). An obvious question would be whether sexually coercive men have higher sexual appetites than noncoercive males. Kafka (2008) has argued that sex offending males do tend to be hypersexual. A first step of defining "hypersexuality" is to examine normative samples in the community and determine level of sexual expression. Kinsey, Pomeroy, and Martin (1948) reported that 7.6% of American males (from adolescence to age 30) had a mean total sexual outlet (TSO)/week, defined as orgasms, seven or more times per week for a period of 5 years. Orgasm from masturbation was the most frequent way of achieving orgasm. In the most recent national survey of sexual behavior (Lauman et al., 1994), 7.6% of American males engaged in sex four or more times per week with a partner for at least one year. Atwood and Gagnon (1987) also surveyed high school and college-aged males and found that 5% of high school students and 3% of college-aged males masturbated on a daily basis. It was also found that 14.5% masturbated two to six time per week for the past year. Using these community surveys, Kafka (2008) defined hypersexuality in males 15 years and older as a TSO/week of seven or more for at least 6 months. Another criterion was that the males had to be sexually preoccupied with sexual fantasies, urges, or behaviors for at least 1–2 hours per day. Langstrom and Hanson (2006) examined a large Swedish sample of males and females (n=2,450) and developed a composite impersonal sex index that included masturbation four or more times per week, frequent pornography use, frequent soliciting of prostitutes, and/or having multiple sex partners. Using this index, hypersexual males tended to be younger, have experienced separation from their parents, lived in urban areas, reported greater diversity of sexual experience, and were more likely to start their sexual behavior at an earlier age. In one study of 220 consecutively evaluated outpatient males seeking treatment for sexual behavior problems, a subgroup with the highest lifetime indicators of hypersexuality were repeat sexual offenders with multiple paraphilias, including voyeurism, exhibitionism, and pedophilia. This group also reported the highest TSO/week (mean=10) and the highest rate of incarceration for sexual offenses (34.6%). Kafka (2003)

Hypersexuality may contribute to sexual violence.

reported that 90% of this subgroup of offenders could be correctly classified if a TSO/week of five was present for a minimum duration of 6 months while maintaining a minimum of one hour/day of time consumed with nonintimate partner-related sexual behaviors.

Other researchers have emphasized the importance of sex drive as an explanatory factor of sexual aggression. Prentky and Burgess (2000) identified strength of sex drive as a risk factor for recidivism of rape and child molestation. Hanson et al. (2003) identified sex drive as a risk factor of recidivism for sex offenders. Knight and Sims-Knight (2003) included sexual drive/preoccupation as an important factor in their structured equation model of coercive sexual behavior against women.

3.3.1   Sexual Coercion and Sex Hormones

Sex hormones, and testosterone in particular, have been identified as part of the biology of hypersexuality. Kafka (2008) emphasizes the role of testosterone in the sexual violence of men against women and children. Functional magnetic resonance imaging (MRI) and positron emission tomography (PET) have demonstrated the effects of testosterone on the forebrain, amygdale, thalamic, and hypothalamic nuclei of the brain, which can influence sexual motivation. Assessment of circulating testosterone in the blood, which is the measure most frequently used, is complicated by the fact that the level fluctuates rapidly due to recent sexual behavior and other factors. High circulating testosterone levels have been more consistently related to irritability, aggression, and violence than sexually coercive behavior (Christensen & Knussman, 1987), but research has indicated higher levels of circulating testosterone in the most sexually violent males compared to less violent sexually coercive males (Kafka, 2008). However, the clearest evidence for the influence of testosterone on sexually aggressive males comes from the effects of surgical or chemical castration (Bradford, 2001). Clearly, surgical and chemical castration with antiandrogens dramatically reduces circulating testosterone, sexual drive, and sexually coercive behavior.

> **The importance of hormones, and in particular circulating testosterone, in sexual violence is seen in the decrease in sexually coercive behavior following surgical and chemical castration.**

3.4   Assessment Strategies

3.4.1   Psychosocial Evaluation

The major portion of this book will focus on treatment. In order to assist the sexually coercive individual in planning appropriate treatment, it is essential that a thorough psychosexual evaluation be completed. Such an evaluation, if it is done properly, will be an important document in planning and guiding treatment. The Association for the Treatment of Sexual Abusers (ATSA) Practice Standards and Guidelines (2005) list important types of information to be included in a good psychosexual evaluation:
- Availability of appropriate community supports
- Access to potential victims

- Criminal and other antisocial behavior and values
- Developmental history and family background
- Deviant sexual interests and arousal
- Education and employment histories
- History of aggression or violence
- History of sexually abusive behavior, including details about victims, tactics used in the commission of the offense, and the circumstances in which the sexual abuse occurred
- Insight into offense precursors and risk
- Level of cognitive functioning and other responsivity factors
- Medical and mental health history
- Official and unreported history of sexual and nonsexual crimes
- Peer and romantic relationship history
- Relevant personality traits such as, but not limited to suspiciousness, hostility, risk-taking, impulsivity, and psychopathology
- Sexual history, including sexual fantasies, urges, and behavior, early sexual experiences, number and duration of sexual relationships, gender identity, and sexual orientation, masturbation, and intercourse frequency, sexual functioning, and unusual sexual interests or behavior that are not sexually deviant or illegal, such as cross-gender dressing
- Substance use
- Use of sexually arousing materials (e.g., magazines, computer pornography, books, videos, Internet sites, telephone services)

This thorough psychosexual evaluation must be based on different sources of information to help assure that reliable conclusions can be reached about the offender. An especially important source of information is the client interview. However, the reliability of self-report information is always suspect in cases of sexual violence, and therefore collaboration of interview findings from multiple sources is important. Interviews with collaterals are important to address many different treatment targets and especially transition planning. These collaterals can include family members, romantic partners, spouses/partners, employers, previous treatment providers, probation/parole officers, etc. Care must always be taken to secure the appropriate release forms that are in compliance with the regulations of the jurisdiction where the offender is being evaluated.

Current standards of practice in treatment of sexually coercive individuals emphasize the importance of assessing deviant sexual interests.

The ATSA standards also list measures of sexual preference or deviant fantasies and/or arousal as being important. These can include psychometric tests such as the Multiphasic Sex Inventory (Nichols & Molinder, 1984), or other measures such as phallometric testing or viewing time, both of which will be discussed below. Card sorts are a promising and innovative way of assessing sexual interests (Laws, 1986).

3.4.2   Psychometric Testing

Psychometric testing can be used to address important aspects of the person's functioning in treatment or to individualize treatment based on assessment results. IQ and everyday functioning ability can be assessed with standardized clinical tools. These measures help assess responsivity to treatment and may underscore the need to modify the program in different ways to accommodate the cognitive skills of the client. Personality traits, such as suspiciousness, hostility, and psychopathy can be measured with the more omnibus personality tests, such as the Multiphasic Personality Inventory II (MMPI-2) or the Millon Clinical Multiaxial Inventory III (MCMI-3). Specific traits and state symptoms can be measured with tools like the Psychopathy Checklist – Revised (PCL-R; Hare, 2003) for psychopathy or numerous self-esteem measures. Other tools can also be used to assess tendencies to repress or malinger.

It is very important to gather and review any official documents such as criminal justice records, witness statements, previous assessment and treatment reports, polygraph reports, medical records, and victim impact statements. Collaboration among data sources is important because exaggerated information or simply false information is sometimes passed along in social histories and other reports. It is always important to have multiple sources of information to verify the self-report of sexually violent individuals.

3.4.3 Risk Assessment

It can be helpful to use risk assessment tools when appropriate norms are available. Three approaches are helpful. The first uses a structured clinical interview with ratings of static, historical factors that can be reliably counted and scored. The second uses a structured interview to assess dynamic or changeable indicators of risk of re-offending. The third approach utilizes empirically guided clinical assessments of both static and dynamic indicators. These tools allow clinician judgment, but guide consideration of both static factors and dynamic factors that have been empirically shown to predict re-offending. Hanson et al. (2003) summarize the research with regard to structured prediction tools and find that the Static-99 (Hanson & Thorton, 2000) was the most accurate predictor of sexual crime recidivism, followed closely by the Rapid Risk Assessment for Sexual Offense Recidivism (RRASOR; Hanson, 1997), the Violence Risk Appraisal Guide (VRAG; Quinsey, Harris, Rice, & Cormier, 1998), and the Sex Offender Risk Appraisal Guide (SORAG; Quinsey et al., 1998). A major criticism of these tools that only use static indicators is that the particular static indicator cannot change and therefore does not have utility in treatment referrals or planning (Doren, 2002; Witt & Conroy, 2009).

> The assessment of dynamic risk indicators can be helpful for treatment because treatment should be directed toward risk indicators that can be improved.

Several new assessment tools utilize the dynamic or changeable factors rather than just static indicators. Hanson and Harris (2000) divided the Sex Offender Need Assessment Rating (SONAR) into two parts that include the Stable-2000 and the Acute-2000. They found that this tool was able to discriminate recidivists from nonrecidivists after controlling for scores on the VRAG and the Static-99.

An example of a general risk assessment tool is the Level of Service Inventory-Revised (LSI-R; Andrews & Bonta, 2001), but the more specific sex offender risk tools are probably more useful, like the Sexual Violence Risk-20 (SVR-20; Boer, Hart, Kropp, & Webster, 1997). Research with this tool has shown predictive power that is just as good as the actuarially developed scales (de Vogel, de Ruiter, van Beck, & Mead, 2004).

3.4.4   Assessment of Sexual Fantasies

It is important to systematically assess sexual deviant fantasies because their presence and strength predict relapse. The most commonly accepted measure of deviant arousal is phallometry or penile plethysmography (PPG). The ATSA standards (2005) indicate that people using phallometry results should be familiar with the process and research on the reliability of findings. The standards indicate that phallometry can be useful for identifying deviant sexual interests during the initial evaluation. It can also be helpful at different stages of treatment to help increase client disclosure and measure changes in sexual arousal patterns over the course of treatment. Some have argued strongly for the validity of phallometry in predicting recidivism (Seto, 2008), whereas others have questioned the reliability of phallometry findings with sex offenders (Looman & Marshall, 2005).

The ATSA standards caution that phallometry is not to be used exclusively for determining deviant sexual interests, but can be used in conjunction with the individual's history of offending behavior and pattern of masturbation. Laboratories doing PPGs should have a standard protocol for fitting the gauges, determining what stimuli to use, and deciding when and how to record and score data. The standards urge that examiners use appropriate stimulus sets to assess sexual interests. Stimulus sets depicting children and adults should be used if you are testing deviant sexual interests of children. There should be at least two examples of each category so that appropriate comparisons could be made to deviant and normal stimuli. Stimulus sets that are more explicit tend to better discriminate between those who offend versus control subjects. The use of neutral scenes can also help with a validity check. Audio tapes of nonconsenting sex and violence can be used in testing for both child and adult deviant interests.

Those examiners who use the PPG should be aware of the applicable legislation in their jurisdiction about the possession and use of sexually explicit materials. Specific informed consent is required for the testing procedure.

The most common ways of scoring plethysmograph data use standardized scores of percentage of full erection and millimeter of circumference change. Research has shown that standardized scores (e.g., z scores) are effective in discriminating between groups. Indices of deviance can be calculated by subtracting the mean peak response to nondeviant stimuli from the mean peak score to deviant stimuli. The ATSA standards give the example of a pedophile index being calculated by subtracting the mean peak response to stimuli depicting adults from the mean peak response to stimuli depicting prepubescent children. The ATSA standards contend that initial deviant sexual interests with phallometric assessment is linked with recidivism and that repeated testing can provide important information on treatment progress.

The accurate assessment of deviant sexual interests is important because it predicts further offenses.

Research suggests that deviant sexual interests are very predictive of sexual offending recidivism. Hanson and Bussiere (1998) found in their meta-analysis of recidivism of sex offenders that phallometry was one of the best predictors of re-offending. However, it is considered one of the most intrusive procedures because it requires an individual to place a sensor around his penis and to listen to sexually explicit stimuli. Because of this intrusiveness, the Ninth Circuit Court of Appeals found in United States v. Weber (2006) that a sex offender could legally refuse the procedure. Witt and Conroy (2009) have reviewed some skeptical critiques of the reliability of PPG and have argued in line with the ATSA standards that PPG should not be used alone to come to a diagnosis of paraphilia. One example of an effort to get around the use of this intrusive procedure is the Screening Scale for Pedophilic Interests (SSPI; Seto & Lalumiere, 2001). This is a short screening tool that consists of the following items: male victim, more than one victim, victim age 11 or younger, unrelated victim. The SSPI correlates highly with PPG results for child molesters. Clearly this is a static screening tool that will not help with assessing treatment progress. Also, the SSPI is not useful for sexual offenders other than child molesters.

Current standards of care emphasize that multiple methods should be used when assessing deviant sexual interests.

3.4.5   Polygraph and Viewing Time Procedures

Another assessment strategy used for treatment purposes is the polygraph. The ATSA standards (2005) identify two treatment goals for the use of the polygraph:
1. Generate information beyond what can be obtained from other self-report measures;
2. Increase compliance with supervision conditions and treatment rules and regulations.

There are four types of postconviction polygraph examinations that are used with sex offenders:
1. Sexual history disclosure tests inquire whether examinees have fully disclosed their sexual history to treatment providers.
2. Maintenance tests seek to verify the degree of compliance with treatment.
3. Monitoring tests check on whether the client has been free of new sex offenses while under supervision.
4. Specific issue tests examine specific questions such as whether the offender attempted to contact the victim or to clarify differences between the client and the victim's report of what occurred.

The ATSA standards (2005) emphasize that caution is needed in using the polygraph with sex offenders. It should not be used as a sole source for making key decisions about the client. The American Polygraph Association and the National Association of Polygraph Examiners have developed standards and certification processes. Certified polygraph administrators should be used, and the standards for using polygraphs with sex offenders need to guide their use. In addition, it is important to be familiar with the laws and state regulations in the jurisdiction where the polygraph is being used. It is also important for treatment personnel to work with the polygrapher in structuring tests that can be reliable, but yet meet the goals of its use for treatment goals. Informed consent should be obtained, including how the information will be used and the possibility of mandated reporting of unknown victims (Witt & Conroy, 2009).

The polygraph can be used to verify self-report and to increase compliance with treatment rules and guidelines.

Using the polygraph does increase the likelihood that clients will provide more information about their offending. However, there is wide variation in the validity and reliability of this information across research studies. Branaman and Gallagher (2005) reviewed the literature and found that the polygraph is increasingly being recommended as a standard for monitoring sex offenders.

However, these authors also report that the research indicates a significant risk of false positive errors with the polygraph. False positive rates increase when questions used in the examination are broad rather than specific. For example, rather than asking about a specific offense or incident, the questions may focus on deviant sexual fantasies or intent. Some have recommended the use of the polygraph in addition to phallometry to assess sexual fantasies, masturbatory practices and past sexual offending behaviors in monitoring those committed for sex offending (Fabian, 2005).

Another specialized assessment used with sex offenders is Viewing Time (Abel, Huffman, Warberg, & Holland, 1998). In this assessment the relative amount of time that clients spend viewing deviant stimuli (e.g., pictures of children who can be clothed, semi-clothed, or nude) is compared to the time that clients spend viewing pictures of more appropriate objects of sexual attention. The ATSA standards indicate that viewing time assessment correlates significantly with self-reported sexual interests and patterns of phallometric responding. However, the standards indicate that not very much information is available about whether testing with this procedure can be helpful with monitoring treatment progress.

Caution is urged by the ATSA standards when using viewing time procedures to assess sexual preferences. The reliability and validity of the test should be known for the population being assessed. Close attention to proper procedures is important. It is essential that a standardized protocol for presenting the stimuli, recording, and scoring results be used. As with the polygraph, information from viewing time should never be used as a sole source of information to make important dispositional or treatment decisions about the client. Informed consent is necessary. Also, as with the other assessments for deviant sexual interests, the clinician must be aware of applicable legislation in the jurisdiction of practice that may apply to the possession and use of sexually explicit stimuli.

Witt and Conroy (2009) are negative about the current empirical support for the use of viewing time. The primary assessment process for viewing time for sex offenders is the Abel Assessment for Sexual Interests (AASI; Abel, Jordan, Hand, Holland, & Phipps, 2001; Abel et al., 1998). Some research has documented poor classification accuracy with juvenile sex offenders and with child molesters (Fischer & Smith, 1999; Smith & Fischer, 1999). In addition, the Massachusetts Court of Appeals in Ready v. Commonwealth (2005) found that the Abel Screen did not meet the Daubert standards for admissibility in court since it lacked empirical validity, was not generally accepted, and had an error rate that was unacceptably high. At this point, it may be too soon to make a determination on the usefulness of the Abel Screen for treatment decisions, before more validity and reliability work is completed.

4

Treatment

I have reviewed the prevalence of sexual violence, diagnoses, attitudes, and beliefs of perpetrators, prognosis, and major theoretical models explaining sexual victimization. These models incorporate direct and indirect influences from variables such as early childhood sexual abuse, family violence, alcohol consumption, and biological predisposing factors. I have briefly reviewed the literature on prevention that has pointed to important targets of intervention. The stage is now set to examine effective treatment strategies. The first task is to ask the basic question of whether treatment of violent sex offenders reduces future victimization of others and improves the life of the offender.

4.1   Does Treatment Work?

The "gold standard" for determining the efficacy of a particular treatment is a clinical trial with random assignment of participants to both a particular treatment condition and a no-treatment or alternative treatment condition. Only with such a controlled experimental approach can extraneous variables that may influence outcomes be controlled. A distinction is often made between "efficacy" and "effectiveness." Efficacy tells us whether a treatment works in a highly controlled experimental situation, whereas effectiveness refers to whether a treatment approach works in real world conditions. A treatment may be efficacious but not effective. This could happen if a highly structured treatment program that is efficacious could not be delivered with fidelity in a real world clinical setting. Generally, an effective program in the real world should demonstrate efficacy in a highly controlled experimental trial (Laws, 2008).

Regardless of the difficulties associated with attempts to actually implement a true randomized design testing treatment of sex offenders, there is some evidence that sex offender treatment results in positive change. Meta-analysis is used to combine research studies that compare sex offender treatment to no treatment. The studies reviewed in meta-analyses are rarely randomized, but no-treatment control groups are used. The important statistic with meta-analysis is the effect size which involves comparing the mean outcome of treated versus untreated groups, adjusted for variability. This involves dividing the reduction of problem behaviors or reduction of future sex crimes by the standard deviation of all the subjects. Cohen (1969) provides the standard that an effect size .20 or better is small but meaningful, whereas an effect size of .50 to .80 is medium, and .80 and above is large.

It is very useful to compare the effect sizes from meta-analyses of treatment of some key physical disorders, mental disorders, and sex offender treatment. This comparison directly addresses the question of whether treatment of sex offenders works compared to the treatment of medical disorders. Marshall (2006a) has performed this comparison with some interesting observations. The effect sizes in a meta-analysis of many studies on aspirin for treatment of myocardial infarction shows positive results with an effect size of .03. Similarly, the effect size for coronary bypass surgery is .15, for chemotherapy for cancer, .08, for neuroleptics for dementia, .37, and AZT for AIDs, .23. Meta-analyses of psychotherapy studies document an effect size of .65 for depression, .51 for public speaking anxiety, and 1.62 for agoraphobia (Marshall, 2006a).

In contrast to the above results, four meta-analyses of treatment for sex offenders have resulted in effect sizes of .24 (Hall, 1995), .43 (Gallagher, Wilson, Hirshfield, Coggeshell, & MacKenzie, 1999), .11 (Hanson et al., 2002), and .13 (Dowden, Antonowicz, & Andrews, 2003). Hanson et al. (2002) computed effect sizes for all kinds of sex offender treatment and then just for cognitive-behavioral treatment, including relapse prevention, and found an effect size of .28 for the later group. This meta-analysis included 49 studies with approximately 9,000 sex offenders assessed in follow-up. It was found across a variety of studies with different release times that untreated sex offenders recidivated at a rate of 16.8% compared to 12.3% for treatment sex offenders. When those programs with clear descriptions that qualified as "cognitive-behavioral" were compared to other treatment programs, the follow-up recidivism rates were even better for the inmates treated with cognitive-behavioral methods (9.9%) compared to other kinds of treatment (17.4%). In the most recent meta-analysis of outcome studies with sex offenders, recidivism rates were found to be very similar to the earlier meta-analysis, and treated inmates were shown to have a recidivism rate of 10.9% compared to 19.2% for untreated sex offenders (Hanson, Bourgon, Helmus, & Hodgson, 2009). If all kinds of recidivism crimes are included and not just sex crimes, then the rates are 31.8% for treated offenders versus 48.3% for comparison groups.

On the basis of these meta-analyses, Marshall (2006a) concluded that sex offenders can be effectively treated. However, not all researchers would agree with this conclusion. Quinsey et al. (1998) compared treated sex offenders to those who refused treatment and those who were judged not to need treatment and concluded that treatment does not work. Those who were judged not to need treatment represented 67% of the control group and most definitely biased these results. The authors dismissed a reanalysis of the same data that found positive results. This reanalysis used a matched control design to help control for the problem of having a control group that were judged to not need treatment (Looman, Abracen, & Nicholaichuk, 2000). Quinsey et al. (1998) also made no attempt to examine the effectiveness of relapse prevention (RP) treatment programs or to delineate different types of treatment that could show differential effectiveness.

This brief overview demonstrates that sex offender treatment does have some effect. This effect is better than many accepted medical treatments, but is not as large as that obtained when psychotherapy is used to treat depression. Some doubt the effectiveness of treatment even in light of these meta-analyses results because a true randomly controlled study has not been performed. In

Meta-analytic research demonstrates that cognitive-behavioral approaches are effective in successfully treating sex offenders.

Treated sex offenders recommit sex crimes at a rate of 10.9% compared to 19.2% for untreated sex offenders.

1981, the state of California ended their Mentally Disordered Sex Offender program and commissioned an experimental treatment program at Atascadero State Hospital for voluntary inmates (Marques, Wiederanders, Day, Nelson, & van Ommeren, 2005). The program, known as the Sex Offender Treatment and Evaluation Project – SOTEP) was designed as a Relapse Prevention Program and continued from 1985 to 1995 with data collection continuing for 6 years after the treatment program ended. Previously, some had argued that treatment of sex offenders did not work (Furby, Weinrott, & Blackshaw, 1989); however, there has been steadily accumulating evidence through large scale summary meta-analyses that treatment of sex offenders does work.

SOTEP represented the attempted implementation of a state-of-the-art Relapse Prevention (RP) program that was believed to be the most efficacious treatment for sex offenders. The treatment was intense with three 90-minute groups that met 3 times each week. The groups were highly structured. In addition, the inmate offenders attended sex education, relaxation training, stress and anger management, and social skills training. Offenders who displayed evidence of deviant sexual fantasies on their phallometric testing were offered behavioral treatment (Marques et al., 2005). All offenders met individually with their clinician/counselor and nursing staff. All activities of therapy, except the individual sessions, were guided by manuals. However, the program designers acknowledged that even though the group sessions were videotaped for random review for supervision purposes, program fidelity was not monitored carefully.

Treatment included cognitive-behavioral and skill-building strategies that focused on reducing the offender's risk of re-offending. Specifically, the goals of the program were to:
1. Increase personal responsibility and consequently reduce the offender's justification of sexual offending;
2. Decrease deviant sexual interest;
3. Teach basic relapse prevention concepts and skills;
4. Improve the ability of offenders to identify high-risk situations for re-offending;.
5. Improve offender skills at avoiding and coping with high-risk situations (Marques et al., 2005).

An experimental design was put in place that included only "volunteers" in the active treatment. A treatment group was established by interviewing eligible offenders in the California Department of Corrections (CDOC) and establishing a group of those who volunteered to be transferred to Atascadero State Hospital to participate in the treatment. Out of this group, approximately half were randomly assigned to be transferred and the other half remained in CDOC where they received standard treatment for alcohol/drug abuse using a RP model. They also attended anger management groups and education groups (this was standard treatment without SOTEP). A second comparison group was formed by using the nonvolunteers who remained in CDOC and likewise received the standard treatment. To make the experimental design more rigorous, the treatment group members that were randomly assigned were matched with offenders in the volunteer comparison group and the nonvolunteer comparison group on age (under or over 40), criminal history (prior felony conviction or not), and type of offense (rapist, molester with male child, molester with fe-

The California Sex Offender Treatment Evaluation Project revealed that a straight relapse-prevention approach to treatment does not work and may make some offenders worse.

male child, or molester with both male and female victims). In addition, child incest offenders and gang rapists were excluded. To be included, the offenders could not have more than two felony convictions prior to the instant offense, had an IQ above 80, and had to be within 18–30 months of release. A number of outcome measures were used including in-treatment measures and recidivism rates (Marques et al., 2005).

The results of this intense, experimentally designed treatment program were disappointing and have been used by some to argue that treatment does not work, and therefore we should spend most of our resources on prediction and control (Seto, 2008). Regardless of the diligence used to set up a true clinical trial with random assignment, there were a number of methodological problems with this effort that limit our ability to draw conclusions about efficacy of the standard treatment of RP. Attrition of subjects became a significant problem, which limits the power of random assignment and matching of subjects. Before the program ever started, 55 out of the 259 assigned RP offenders withdrew and were not transferred to the hospital. After the program started, an additional 37 dropped out before one year of treatment. In order to compensate for this attrition, the designers made every effort to assure program completion, including leaving clients who were not motivated in groups (Marques et al., 2005).

The final data revealed that those who completed at least one year of RP treatment did not differ from the two comparison groups in terms of recidivism after approximately 8.4 years of follow-up in the community. Those who completed at least one year of treatment had a sex re-offense rate of 21.6% compared to 20% for the voluntary control group and 19.1% for the nonvoluntary control group. Those who completed RP also had just as many re-offenses for violent and nonviolent offenses as the comparison groups (16.3% versus 11.6% for the volunteers and 15.0% for the nonvolunteer comparison group) (Marques et al., 2005). All the groups included approximately 70% child molesters and 27% rapists.

The researchers analyzed the data to determine if there were some variables that might be contributing to their failure to document any differences between groups. However, there were no differences when looking at time to re-offend between the groups, except those who dropped out of treatment after starting were more likely to re-offend earlier and had more offenses overall across time. There also were no differences based on type of victim. There were no differences based on static risk indicators of the three groups based on seven items from the Static 99. The seven items included prior sex offenses, convictions for noncontact sex offenses, any unrelated victims, any stranger victims, any male victims, youth of the offender, and never married (Marques et al., 2005).

The researchers have critically looked at the results of this intense study and have made some observations that are important in terms of identifying what does not work and therefore suggesting what might work (Marques et al., 2005). First, randomization was compromised in several ways. For example, only volunteers were eligible to enter the program, and only inmates who admitted to their crimes were accepted into the program. If an inmate had two or more felonies, he could not be in the program. In addition, there was no external incentive for the inmates, and this resulted in high attrition rates once the program began and in the acknowledgement that some unmotivated inmates remained in treatment. In addition, those who were in the comparison groups did receive treatment and, in fact, received RP for substance abuse and treatment for anger. Even though this study had random assignment and matching, those not in the treatment condition did receive RP and other forms of treatment, which compromises this design and means that little can be said about the efficacy of RP from this study. Finally, another reason for these negative findings could be that the location of treatment was very different because all RP inmates were sent to a maximum security mental hospital whereas the comparison group remained in prison. The treatment environment can be assumed to be very different in those two settings.

Other problems also are apparent. We know from the research literature that process variables and therapist behaviors contribute more to positive gains in treatment than treatment strategy per se. The designers of SOTEP acknowledge that the therapists raised the issue that since this was a manual driven program they did not have the flexibility to respond as therapeutically as they sometimes felt that they should. Little was said about therapist and clinician training. In fact, the designers admit that incorporating therapist process training, similar to that emphasized in motivational interviewing, could have made a difference (Marques et al., 2005).

The designers also speculate that the intervention may have been too intense for low to medium risk inmates (Nicolaichuk, Gordon, Gu, & Wong, 2000). In comparison to other recognized successful programs (Marshall, Marshall, Serran, & Fernandez, 2006), the Sex Offender Treatment and Evaluation Project was especially intense, and the intensity may have been counterproductive, especially given clear indications of ambivalence and lack of motivation to change from some of the inmates. The designers acknowledged that aftercare interviews revealed that some inmates did not accept the basic goals of self-control and relapse prevention. This suggests that the RP model, which focuses on avoidance goals, was not acceptable to some offenders. There was also little in the way of preparation to assess and assure that inmates were at a stage of readiness to change their thinking and behavior.

It is also important to mention that a second clinical trial with random assignment has failed to find positive differences between RP strategies and comparison groups (Schweitzer & Dwyer, 2003). Like the SOTEP program, this study had random assignment to treatment representing standard elements of RP. The comparison groups included dropouts and nonparticipants. Similar to SOTEP, there were no differences on recidivism after 5 years of follow-up.

4.2 Reformulated Relapse Prevention

These studies have led some of the original authors who adapted RP from the substance abuse treatment arena to reformulate RP utilizing more current theories and research (Laws & Ward, 2006). These theorists raise the possibility that RP's focus on relapse and deviant behavior makes re-offending too visible and tempting. Even though this idea seems counterintuitive, there is some evidence from reactance theory (Brehm & Brehm, 1981) that this

A focus on relapse and deviant sexual interests may make re-offending too tempting as suggested by psychological reactance theory.

can occur. Others have focused on the importance of self-regulation and the associated emotions that are important for improving self-regulation (Marshall et al., 2006). Even though not intended, the original formulation of RP was cognitive-behavioral and emotion regulation was not emphasized. In the self-regulation reformulation of RP, there is recognition that there are different types of dysfunctional self-regulation. People can have problems with emotion regulation that are associated with tendencies of disinhibition with both positive and negative goals. People can also have problems with behavior controls and have adequate emotion regulation, but fail to pick appropriate strategies for behavioral control. Finally, sometimes people have the wrong goals, whether disinhibition or misregulation is present.

4.3   Different Pathways and Different Treatments

Ward and Hudson (2006) describe four possible pathways to sex offending that more adequately covers the diversity of offending than the rationale presented in RP. These pathways describe different type of goals present for sex offenders and the selection of self-regulation strategy. The avoidant-passive pathway includes offenders who do not control their deviant behavior because of under-regulation or difficulties with disinhibition. The avoidant-active pathway describes those offenders who may have the ability to self-regulate, but who choose strategies that may actually increase the likelihood of re-offending. This is a misregulation pathway. A third type of disinhibited pathway is described as approach-automatic. This pathway is represented by offenders who have behavioral scripts that seem very impulsive and unplanned. This is clearly an under-regulated type of offender. Finally, there is the approach-explicit pathway where the offenders plan and these plans are explicit and sometimes detailed. Self-regulation is intact and the primary problem is setting appropriate goals. The concept of disinhibition does not fit because these individuals do not loose control, nor do they use sexual violence to escape emotional negative states. They seek to maintain a high emotional state during their sex offending.

Relapse prevention has not recognized the complexity of sexual offending. Each of the pathways proposed by Ward and Hudson (2006) would require different strategies for successful treatment. Not all sex offending is due to problems of disinhibition. Thus, important treatment components need to be added to the older RP model. These include working with offenders to establish approach goals, broad work on skills training to increase the probability of achieving important life goals, working on motivation to change, and a focus on emotion-regulation and skill building. In light of SOTEP and more recent thinking, the focus of treatment should include the identification of important life goals and the resources and competencies for the offenders to achieve these goals. Treatment also needs to address more than simple risk management. As Laws and Ward (2006) have indicated, it is likely that RP has devoted too much time to talking about risk and coping, and not enough time to teaching coping skills.

4.4   A Treatment Program That Does Work

It is helpful to consider a sex offender treatment program that has been in development for approximately 38 years in the Canadian federal prison (Marshall et al., 2006). This program is important because of its success and because its designers have through many years researched different components of the program with the goal of demonstrating and improving its effectiveness. The outcome data document a very effective program with the primary outcome being the reduction of recidivism. Out of a total of 614 sex offenders treated in this program and released, follow-up data are available on 534, including 352 child molesters and 182 rapists. After 5.4 years being at-risk of recidivism in the community, only 17 of these offenders were re-arrested. This is a remarkable 3.2% recidivism rate for sex crime re-arrests. Of these 17 offenders, 14 were child molesters and 3 were rapists. The base rate of re-offending for all released offenders in the Canadian federal correctional system is 13.6% for sex offenses and 40% for nonsexual offenses. The authors have speculated that these base rates are similar to those in other parts of the United States.

> The most successful known sex offender treatment program is that found in the Canadian federal prison system. This program reports a 3.2% recidivism rate compared to 13.6% recidivism for untreated sex offenders and 40% for nonsexual criminal offenders.

Because of these impressive results and because this is an evidence-based program that utilizes the latest research, we will describe some of the basic treatment strategies used in this program. The program is generally described as a cognitive-behavioral program that emphasizes therapist skills and approach goals for inmates. It can also be described as a reformulated relapse prevention modal.

4.5   Important Therapist Skills

Before we use this program as a guide to present treatment strategies, readers need to understand what is known about therapist skills and those process variables that can so dramatically affect whether treatment goals are achieved. Unless therapists are skilled in their communication with clients, no strategy will work. It is clear that the skills needed to successfully treat sex offenders are similar to those skills needed for successful outcomes with general psychotherapy. One major criticism of the SOTEP program by the therapists themselves was that they did not have flexibility to work with clients based on individual needs (Marques et al., 2005). Because of countertransference issues or the anxiety we may have in working with someone who sexually abuses others, and especially children, we may find comfort in searching out techniques and strategies rather than focusing on the therapeutic alliance. Ackerman and Hilsonroth (2003) conducted a meta-analysis of therapist characteristics that influence positive outcomes from psychotherapy. Overall, 25% of the variance of therapeutic gain in general psychotherapy research was due to the therapeutic alliance. Another meta-analysis of 79 therapy studies found an effect size of .22 for the therapeutic alliance (Martin, Garske, & Davis, 2000). Sex offender treatment can be provided within a therapy group or individually, even though, generally, group therapy is considered the preferred mode. It is striking that 40% of the variance of outcome in group therapy can be attributed to cohesiveness and expressiveness of the group (Beech & Fordham, 1997). What is

> As much as 40% of the variance in treatment outcome with sex offenders can be attributed to cohesiveness and expressiveness of the group.

important for clients is having someone who understands them, who instills hope and who offers encouragement. The quality of the therapeutic alliance and group cohesiveness and expressiveness are part of the foundation upon which all successful psychological treatment of sexually violent individuals occurs.

Marshall et al. (2003) have argued that effective therapists always have five goals when treating sex offenders: (1) They create an appropriate alliance with the client; (2) They evoke from the client a belief that change is possible; (3) They provide an opportunity to learn; (4) They instill in the clients an expectation that they can derive benefits from treatment; and (5) They emotionally engage the clients. This approach is based on the work of earlier humanistic psychologists who argued for the necessary therapist characteristics of genuineness, empathy, understanding, and warmth. A manual driven therapeutic program that does not emphasize these key therapist characteristics will never work.

In real practice, sex offender treatment tends to be confrontational. In fact, some have argued that forming a therapeutic alliance with sex offenders is not appropriate and that strong confrontation is essential with sex offender treatment (Salter, 1988). However, Marshall et al. (2003) have argued that such an approach ignores psychotherapy research that shows that clients who are ambivalent about change do not respond positively to confrontation. Many sex offenders are resistant, ambivalent about change, and tend to minimize the harm that results from their conduct. DiClemente (1991) would place most sex offenders in the precontemplation stage of change and confrontation is especially damaging to progress for these individuals. Fernandez (2006) has argued that gains of sex offender clients exposed to confrontational therapy are superficial and do not generalize outside of treatment. Patterson and Forgatch (1985) argue that noncompliance with psychological treatment increases significantly as confrontation in therapy increases. Being positive in treatment is important and underscores all other essential elements of effective treatment. There are other different therapist characteristics and behaviors that have been shown to be important to achieving positive outcomes in treatment. Before reviewing strategies in treatment, I will review these therapist variables, so that therapists can reflect on how effectively they demonstrate these characteristics.

4.5.1   Empathy

It is important for therapists to have empathy for their clients, even though this is sometimes difficult with clients who are sex offenders. Orlinsky et al. (1994) found in a review of 47 psychotherapy studies that 34 studies reported that ratings of therapist empathy correlated significantly with treatment outcome. Likewise, as much as 67% of the variance in effectiveness of treatment with problem drinkers has been attributed to independent ratings of accurate empathy displayed by the therapist (Miller, Taylor, & West, 1980). Fernandez (2002) has edited a book on empathy in therapy for sex offenders. The title of her book is *In Their Shoes*, which hints at a working definition of empathy. Marshall (2002) proposes a four-stage model of empathy that applies to therapists and offenders. The first component is the ability to accurately perceive the emotional state of another person. The second component involves the ability to see things as another sees them. The third component of this model is the capacity to respond emotionally to the other person's distress. Finally, the last component is the enactment of some compassionate response or sympathy.

How do therapists develop accurate empathy skills and can training help? Observers of empathic therapists describe these therapists as people who can communicate to their clients that they take the relationship seriously. This is done through their body language and their tone of voice. They make eye contact, lean forward, use open body language, and nod and reflect upon what the client says in a warm and friendly tone (Fernandez & Serran, 2002). Bachelor (1988) has suggested that there are four different types of empathy that help clients in different ways. The first type is cognitive (or facilitative) empathy and involves a reformulation or interpretation of what the client says in order to help the client gain perspective. It is important with this type of empathy that the therapist understands accurately the inner world of the client and his ongoing thoughts and emotions. If the therapist accurately reflects back to the client his thinking and "mirrors" the client's communication in a nonjudgmental way, then this type of empathy will increase self-disclosure, self-understanding, and positive change. The second type of empathy is called affective empathy. The client comes to see that the therapist understands his feelings and emotions. The therapist acknowledges the client's feelings and asks open-ended questions to help clarify these feelings. The third type of empathy is labeled sharing. The primary effect of this type of empathy is to communicate to the client that others experience their emotions as well and that there are solutions. Some disclosure and use of "I feel" statements by the therapist can show that the therapist is experiencing in the moment with the client. The fourth type of therapist empathy is called nurturant empathy. Therapists displaying this type of empathy are attentive, caring, and protective.

The classic description of empathy is by Carkhuff and Pierce (1975) who define five different levels of empathy based on the sophistication of the therapist. Level 1 is a lack of empathy. Here the therapist may give reassurance or advice opposed to what the client is saying. The client may feel that the therapist really does not understand them or is not accepting of their feelings. Level 2 empathy involves focusing on just the content and ignoring the feelings. Level 3 involves just repeating the feelings expressed by the client, but not adding anything (e.g., Client: "I feel really depressed right now." Therapist: "I understand that you are really feeling depressed."). Level 4 adds something new in the reflection on the client's emotions (e.g., Client: "How am I going to survive without him?" Therapist: "I can see that it is hard for you to see any hope right now."). Finally, Level 5 adds something new and suggests an action step for the client to consider (e.g., Therapist: "You express hopelessness and uncertainty right now. But I am impressed by how well you have coped up to this point. What have you been doing to do as well as you have done?"). To be effective in therapy, Carkhuff and Pierce indicate that the therapist must be operating at Level 3 or higher.

It does seem possible to train therapists to be empathic (Zucker, Worthington, and Forsyth, 1985). Fernandez (2002) describes a training approach for therapists that assumes that an empathic relationship between the client and therapist is facilitated when the therapist is able to take the perspective of the client

The primary implication of research on outcomes and therapist factors is that therapists need to be specifically trained to be able to effectively work with sexually violent persons.

(i.e., perceive the world as the client would perceive it) and demonstrates a number of communications skills such as active listening and reflecting. Empathy training is conducted in groups of 8 to 10 and where each participant role-plays a therapist and then does a role-reversal and role-plays a client. The others in the group provide those taking the role of a therapist feedback on the empathy skills that they practiced. At the end of 24 hours of training, the trainer then assesses each therapist on a therapist criteria scale. In order to be a primary therapist with sex offender groups in Fernandez's treatment program, the person must obtain a high score on this scale. If this score is not achieved, then a therapist must work as a secondary therapist and must be with a primary therapist at all times, and receive feedback until they can progress in their therapeutic skills. This role-play experiential approach to therapist empathy training would also apply to other therapist skills.

4.5.2   Genuineness

Marshall et al. (2003) identified genuineness as the second therapist skill linked to positive outcomes of treatment with sex offenders. This quality is present when the therapists are nondefensive, comfortable with themselves, and therefore capable of being involved and interested in the group members. A similar characteristic is the ability to show respect, which has been shown to predict treatment outcome (Rabavilas, Boulougouris, & Perissaki, 1979). Psychotherapy research has generally shown client ratings of genuineness of the therapist to be positively correlated to outcome (Orlinsky et al., 1994).

4.5.3   Warmth

A third therapist skill is the ability to show warmth to clients. This means that the therapist comes across as accepting, caring, and supportive. Of course, this does not mean that the therapist ever communicates acceptance of hurtful behavior, but rather acceptance of the person. Research has persistently shown a positive link between ability of the therapist to communicate acceptance of the person and positive feelings of the clients and positive outcomes (Orlinsky et. al, 1994).

4.5.4   Acceptance

Another important therapist skill is the ability to communicate acceptance of the client, even though the person may have committed a violence act. In the Vanderbilt Psychotherapy Project, Hans Strupp (1980) found that disrespect- ful therapist responses to defensive statements made by clients predicted poor outcomes. Premature and early client dropouts from therapy have been linked to clients feeling that their therapist did not respect them and did not understand their problems (Saltzman, Luetgert, Roth, Creaser, & Howard, 1976). In regard to sex offenders, this requires that the therapist have the ability to separate acceptance of the person from the harmful acts the person may have committed.

4.5.5   Confidence

Psychotherapy research has consistently shown that good outcomes are positively correlated with clients' ratings of therapist credibility and confidence (Seligman, 1990). Likewise, Ryan, and Gizynski (1971) found that improvement in therapy was linked to therapist confidence. Frank (1971) stated that confidence in the therapist was an essential element of therapy. McGuff, Gitlin, and Enderlin (1996) found that even steady attendance at therapy was related to client ratings of therapist confidence.

4.5.6   Supportiveness

Therapists, whether in group or individual sessions, must be able to offer support to the client. We know from solid research that self-efficacy expectations of the clients are important for therapeutic progress. But many sex offenders have low self-esteem, contrary to what many professionals and the public believe, and therefore these individuals do not think that they have the coping skills to positively change. Thus, the therapist must be skilled at reinforcing positive and effective behaviors to enhance the self-efficacy of the clients for progress. This therapist behavior is present when the therapist engages in active listening, positive evaluation, encouragement, and comforting statements. Improved self-efficacy in clients has been linked to clients' positive perceptions of the therapist and the perception that therapy sessions are supportive and worthwhile (Fuller & Hill, 1985).

4.5.7   Emotional Expressivity

One component of any successful psychotherapeutic approach is the expression of emotions by clients during treatment. Interpersonal schemas or mindsets represent a combination or fusion of emotions and cognitions. Some of these negative schemas are important targets in treatment of sex offenders, such as attitudes toward women and children's sexuality. The encouragement and expression of emotions in therapy is directly related to therapy outcome (Cooley & LaJoy, 1980; Orlinsky et. al, 1994). We also know that the expression of emotions by clients is linked to the expression of emotion by therapists (Saunders, 1999). One of the shortcomings of RP was the lack of focus on emotion expression in therapy and the learning of emotion self-regulation skills. This could be a key reason why standard RP programs have not been shown to be efficacious in clinical trials. The therapist should model the expression of emotions in a coping manner for the clients; this will help empower clients to express emotions and develop emotion regulation skills.

4.5.8   Self-Disclosure

Another closely related therapist skill is self-disclosure. Mahoney (1974) argues that therapists need to use self-disclosure to demonstrate that coping is possible and mastery of emotions and behaviors can be achieved. When therapists present their own stresses and struggles to cope, then this encourages clients to accept themselves and begin to set realistic goals. The therapist must be careful in self-disclosure not to take the focus off the group members, since too much therapist disclosure can decrease confidence in the therapist.

4.5.9   Open-Ended Questions

Effectiveness research has shown that cognitive-behavioral approaches with sex offenders are the treatments of choice. At the heart of cognitive-behavioral approaches is cognitive restructuring. Questions about their thoughts and emotions are essential to help the clients change their thinking and emotions. The type and manner of questions used in treatment is important. Research has shown that clients respond more openly and with more insight when open-ended questions are used (Barkman & Shapiro, 1986).

4.5.10   Flexibility of Style

The literature reviewed above suggests that a nondirective approach is the best strategy; however, considerable research suggests that a balance between therapist directiveness and nondirectiveness is needed when treating sex offenders. Structure, and therefore directiveness, is helpful in promoting problem solving and enhances the likelihood of cooperation in therapeutic homework (Elliott, Barker, Caskey, & Pistrang, 1982; Schaap, Brennun, Schindler, & Hoogduin, 1993), but a correlation has also been found between therapist directiveness and negativity and resistance from clients (Schaap et al., 1993). In a study that is over a half-century old, Ashby, Ford, Gueney and Gueney (1957) found that a reflective style of therapy was better with defensive and aggressive clients, while a more directive therapist style led to better outcomes for clients that were nondefensive and more confident. Therapists need to be flexible in their interactive styles based on different needs of clients. When complex problems are being presented by clients, a nondirective approach may be important for progress (Beutler, Pollack, & Jobe, 1978). Even the same clients may require different approaches at different times.

4.5.11   Positive Attitudes

All therapist skills should be directed at encouraging active participation of clients in treatment. Active participation has consistently been shown to be associated with higher probability of completing treatment and having successful outcomes (Garfield & Bergin, 1986; Gomes-Schwartz, 1978; Strupp & Hadley, 1979). When therapists are able to encourage clients to display active listening, complete homework assignments, and participate actively, then positive outcomes are more likely (Safran & Segal, 1990). It is more likely that active participation will occur if therapists are positive in their approach with clients and clients have positive goals that are central in therapy (Emmons,

1996). This important principle applies regardless of the nature of the client behavioral problem, and most clearly to sex offender treatment.

4.5.12 Rewarding

The therapist must also be skilled at rewarding positive client behaviors in therapy. Rewarding statements of goal-oriented behavior from therapist to depressed patients was associated with client improvement (Fuchs & Rehm, 1977). It is especially important to reward change talk, as is becoming more apparent from the literature on motivational interviewing (Amrhein, Miller, Yahne, Palmer, & Fulcher, 2003). Coping skills vary considerably with sex offenders, and therefore it is important for the therapist to break down tasks into manageable steps so that opportunities to reward are present. This process is similar to behavioral chaining. Therapeutic homework assignments provide an opportunity for rewarding feedback to the clients.

4.5.13 Humor

Humor can also be very therapeutic. The use of humor in therapy can reduce client anxiety, feelings of inferiority, and help clients recognize the value of humor in their own lives (Falk & Hill, 1992). Humor can contribute to a therapeutic alliance between the client and therapist. However, it is important to be cautious about the type of humor that is expressed. Sarcasm can be perceived by the client as demeaning and is often misinterpreted as the therapist belittling clients.

Most psychotherapy research with different client populations, including sex offenders, has found the importance of these therapist skills to be as robust in contributing to positive outcomes as the particular strategy of therapy used (Marshall et al., 2003). But there is also evidence that some therapist communication styles may contribute to negative effects in treatment. These negative therapist characteristics can include being overly confrontive, showing rejection, manipulation of the client, low interest, being critical, sarcastic, hostile or angry, showing discomfort with the client, being unresponsive, dishonest, judgmental, authoritarian, and defensive (Marshall et al., 2003).

4.6 Support Versus Confrontation Versus Collusion

Well-intentioned therapists in sex offender treatment unfortunately use one particular negative therapist communication style far too often. This approach is aggressive confrontation. Anna C. Salter (1988), a recognized expert in the field of sexual violence, has advocated that strong confrontation is essential with sex offenders and that a psychotherapeutic approach is inappropriate. The acceptance of this approach is understandable because of the extreme nature of the offenses committed, and the clear cognitive distortions and defenses of the offenders. In addition, some therapists may feel it is important that they not

Research has shown that aggressive confrontation with sex offenders leads to negative outcomes.

appear to tolerate sexual offenses. However, if the goal of therapy is to reduce sex offending, aggressive confrontation may actually be counterproductive.

Yalom and Lieberman (1971) describe aggressive confrontation in group therapy as being harmful. One reason why aggressive confrontation may be especially harmful for sex offenders is that they may not be at a stage of readiness for change and are very defensive. Diclemente (1991) indicates that confrontation when clients are at a preliminary stage of precontemplation can be harmful. A confrontation approach with clients with substance abuse problems has been found to actually increase the likelihood of client drinking in one-year follow-up (Miller, Benefield, & Tonigan, 1993). Annis and Chan (1983) found that a confrontational approach was especially damaging to offenders with low self-esteem, and many sex offenders have both substance abuse problems and low self-esteem. Beech and Fordham (1997) found similar negative outcomes with the use of a confrontational approach with sex offenders. Recent research with sex offenders has demonstrated that a confrontational approach specifically with sex offenders increases defensiveness and thus reduces gains in treatment (Beech & Hamilton-Giachritsis, 2005; Drapeau, 2005). Such a confrontational approach is sometimes justified for reasons of being "honest" with the clients and not being "soft" with this especially manipulative population. Cormier and Cormier (1991) found that when clients are faced with a forceful therapist they will typically: (1) discredit or vigorously challenge the therapist; (2) devalue the issue; or (3) acquiesce and then dismiss the issue as irrelevant. In an important study, Patterson and Forgatch (1985) found that clients were significantly more noncompliant as the degree of confrontation increased.

The question naturally arises, how can you change negative and harmful behavior if you do not challenge the perpetrator? However, challenging irrational beliefs and cognitive distortions in a supportive manner while rewarding small steps of positive change is very different than strong confrontation, as is commonly practiced in prisons and probation and parole offices around the US. Current research suggests we are enhancing the probability of future offending by using aggressive confrontation.

A supportive and rewarding approach is not the same as colluding with sexual offenders.

It is important to emphasize that a supportive, nonconfrontational approach with sex offenders is not the same as a collusive approach. Fernandez (2006) defines a collusive approach as one that encourages a sex offender's "distorted, exculpatory and self-protective views of his offenses" (p. 190). Therapists can be overly compassionate and have difficulties challenging and setting boundaries. Collusive therapists tend to view their clients as victims and may have difficulties insisting that their clients take responsibility for their harmful actions. These therapists may have a need to be liked by their clients and are uncomfortable challenging in a firm but still supportive manner. They implicitly may take responsibility for their clients' actions and unintentionally encourage clients to believe that their behavior is beyond their control. The therapist skills described above do not require that the therapist collude with the perpetrator or condone his harmful actions.

Before examining therapeutic strategies for sex offender treatment, we need to consider in more detail two important concepts involved in therapeutic change. These concepts are therapeutic alliance and group cohesion. Martin, Garske, and Davis (2000) published a meta-analysis of results of 79 studies on therapeutic alliance. Three different components were used to define therapeutic alliance: (1) the emotional bond between the client and the therapist; (2) the collaborative nature of the relationship; and (3) agreement about the goals of treatment. The effect size for the role of therapeutic alliance alone ($r = .22$) in this meta-analysis is about equal to psychotherapy outcomes in general and positive outcomes for cognitive-behavioral treatment for sex offenders. Another meta-analysis of therapeutic alliance found a very similar result (Hovath & Symonds, 1991). It is clear that positive therapeutic alliance is associated with positive outcomes and that a negative therapeutic alliance is associated with negative outcomes and not just the absence of positive outcomes (Marzialli & Alexander, 1991). In a corrections setting, poor therapeutic alliance may lead to negative outcomes that increase recidivism in sexually violent offenders. Good therapist skills that can be established and encouraged through training and supervision, and positive therapeutic alliances will result in positive outcomes.

The second related concept necessary for understanding the linkbetween therapeutic strategy and outcome is group cohesion. Similar to therapeutic alliance, the definition of group cohesion involves the clients and therapists working together with support and collaboration. Beech and Fordham (1997) used the Moos Group Environment scale with sex offender group treatment in different clinical settings and found that the greater the group cohesion, as rated by the clients, the greater the improvement on measures of progress in therapy.

Group cohesion involves the clients and therapists working together with support and collaboration.

4.7 Motivational Interviewing

One overall therapeutic approach that emphasizes these therapeutic skills is motivational interviewing (MI) (Arkowitz & Miller, 2008). One of the retrospective conclusions of the designers of the SOTEP program was that they should have utilized motivational interviewing to address the lack of motivation on the part of some offenders (Marquez et. al, 2005). Motivational interviewing can be used as a primary treatment strategy, as it is in the Swedish prison system (Farbring & Johnson, 2008), or it can be used to guide other therapeutic strategies with the idea that its techniques will make other therapeutic approaches more effective. Thus, it can be used at intake or throughout therapy.

One of the key assumptions of MI is that clients are ambivalent about change and that their motivation to change may become stronger or weaker at different points of therapy. A central goal of MI is to increase intrinsic motivation of the clients by emphasizing goals and values that the client accepts rather than those imposed from someone else through persuasion, threats, or coercing the person to change. One key argument of MI is that there can be a paradoxical decrease in the desire to change and externally imposed goals can actually produce an effect that is the exact opposite to that which is intended. Experimental research with children is used to show the importance of intrinsic motivation rather than externally driven motivation. For example, children who are observed playing with their favorite toys will actually decrease their play time with their favorite toys if they are praised for playing with those toys (Lepper, Greene, & Nisbett, 1973). Likewise, the work of Davidson and Valins

(1969) demonstrates that changes that are attributed to oneself are more likely to endure. The similarity of the rationale of MI with recent theories regarding stages of readiness to change is apparent.

Prochaska and Norcross (2004) have labeled five stages of readiness to change as precontemplation, contemplation, preparation, action, and maintenance. The psychotherapy literature has always addressed "resistance" in clients, but MI attempts to facilitate positive change and prefers the more positive term motivation. If clients are pressured or cajoled to change when they are not at a stage of readiness to change, then an aversive reaction may occur. The work of Brehm and Brehm (1981) is important in understanding negative outcomes. People can experience an aversive reactance state when they perceive a threat to their personal freedom and may even react oppositionally when directed to change. Prochaska and Prochaska (1991) maintain that resistance and noncompliance will result when there is a mismatch between a stage of readiness to change and the therapy process.

A central goal of MI is to increase intrinsic motivation of clients by emphasizing goals and values that they accept rather than those imposed through persuasion, threats, or coercion.

The intent of MI is for the therapist to work collaboratively with the client, promote autonomy, and evoke the client behaviors necessary for positive change. MI is a client-centered approach founded on the work of Carl Rogers. The therapist helps to promote positive change by exploring and resolving client ambivalence (Miller & Rollnick, 2002). The goal is to create a therapeutic environment where the client becomes the agent for change. Thus, there are four basic assumptions of MI. First, clients in therapy are ambivalent about change. Second, clients change in their motivation levels throughout treatment. Third, therapists should be attuned to these variations in motivation and ambivalence. Fourth and finally, intrinsic motivation follows from positive goals and values that are important to the client rather than externally imposed.

There are five basic communication skills needed by therapists using motivational learning. First, the therapist should use open-ended questions so that the client does most of the talking. Second, reflective listening is critical and has been described as the "single most important skill" (Arkowitz et al., 2008, p. 7). Third, the therapist's communication needs to affirm the client as a person and efforts that the client makes toward change. This occurs through the expression of appreciation and understanding. Fourth, the therapist uses summary statements to show the client that they have listened. Summary statements also allow the therapist to reinforce change talk of the client. Finally, the therapist elicits change talk from the client. Change talk involves client statements of desire, perceived ability, need, readiness, reasons, or commitment to change. The therapist must be skilled at quickly recognizing these types of statements and responding with reinforcement. Psychotherapy research has shown that client statements made in sessions reflecting commitment to change were the strongest predictors for outcome in drug use (Amrhein et al., 2003). The therapist is readily seen as an advocate for change.

Besides the five communication skills, there are eight other MI skills that have been described by Arkowitz et al. (2008): (1) The therapist must be accepting of the assumption that collaboration with the client is important for eliciting motivation from the client. For some therapists who are directive and who feel an obligation to teach and instruct, this assumption is difficult. (2) The therapist must have client-centered skills and especially empathy. These skills can be enhanced through training, supervision, and assessment of feedback from clients. (3) The therapist must be able to recognize change talk. (4) Once expressed, the change talk needs to be reinforced by the therapist, and therefore the clinician must have the skills to reinforce clients for their change talk. (5) Clinicians must have skills necessary to minimize resistance. Motivation is a function of the client's values and goals, and, in particular, the discrepancy between their current status and behaviors, and what they want in life. The therapist needs to have the skills to help the client explore their own reasons for change and overcoming resistance. (6) The therapist needs to have good judgment about when clients are ready to formulate a change plan. MI contends that premature formulation of a change plan can have the unintended result of increasing commitment to the status quo. (7) The clinician should elicit commitment from the client to implement the plan. (8) Finally, the MI clinician needs to be flexible and apply these skills as an introduction and as an adjunct to other strategies.

Miller, Yahne, Moyers, Martinez, and Pirritano (2004) have conducted research on the effectiveness of a two to three day training program to enhance these skills. This research has not been able to document that clients respond differently to therapists who have attended this training versus those who have not. This suggests that MI skills are not as easy to learn as may appear on the surface. The goals of this training were to teach attendees to recognize the differences between reflective listening and other clinician responses, to enable the clinician to be able to have their counseling communications to be at least 50% reflective listening responses, to recognize change talk and to develop skills to reinforce change talk. According to Miller et al. (2004), these skills are complex and require ongoing training and supervision. The University of Arizona has developed a one-year practicum for clinical psychology students that is built around motivational interviewing.

A practical and impressive system application of MI is found in the Swedish Prison System (Farbring & Johnson, 2008). The Swedish prison system in 2003 and 2004 began to place more emphasis on "what works" correctional programs. The majority of the push for implementation of these programs was represented by training and implementation of MI. This initiative was based on a growing body of outcome research showing significant improvement in a number of disorders and problem behaviors after even brief exposure to MI (Hettema, Steele, & Miller, 2005). Good effect sizes for positive change have been found in a number of meta-analyses (Burke, Arkowitz, & Menchola, 2003). Arkowitz and Westra (2002) have argued that MI can be effectively used as a pretreatment to enhance the outcomes of other therapies or can be used within different treatment therapies when ambivalence is present. Even as a pretreatment, comparative research has shown MI to be more effective in enhancing the positive outcomes of cognitive-behavioral therapy than a role-induction technique (Frank, 1974) that includes discussion of the rationale for therapy and the expectations of the therapist and client. The Swedish prison program designers recognized the demonstrated effectiveness of MI in the treatment of substance abusers and especially those who had demonstrated resistance to change and those with high levels of anger.

The Swedish MI program consists of 5 sessions of MI with inmates who are recruited with brochures offering an opportunity "to talk confidentially with a counselor and to help counselors understand how inmates are thinking about their future." A precounseling meeting is scheduled where inmates fill out scales indicating their willingness to change. In session #1, the inmate is provided feedback from the initial assessment meeting with interaction with the client on the nature of change for them personally. Discussion occurs about how change has occurred for them and/or their friends and/or family. The client is encouraged to think about what stage of change is descriptive of them. In session #2, the focus is on determining the client's stage of change, and clients are asked to assign emotional weights to arguments for and against change.Other simple scales are used to help the client assess their perceived importance of change, confidence, priorities, and internal and external motivation for changing their lives. Session #3 involves having the client complete the values card sort (Miller & Mount, 2001), and they are encouraged to write down their most important values in a workbook. Clients are asked to identify discrepancies between these values and their current behavior. This is done in order to help clients elicit change talk. Session #4 involves a discussion with the client of the balance between external and internal motivation that was presented in an earlier session. Two exercises are used in this session. A social network map is used to key relationships in the person's life, and cognitive restructuring is used to reframe negative feedback from family and other significant persons in the client's life. The final session involves work to help the client reframe events in his life that represent failure. This session also has an important exercise that involves the client writing down all the good qualities and resources he possesses. One important goal of this last session is to end in a positive note regarding change talk (Arkowitz & Miller, 2008).

> Five sessions of motivational interviewing with all inmates in the Swedish prison system led to positive changes in attitudes about alcohol/drug use, self-efficacy, and internal motivation.

Virtually all staff and counselors in the Swedish prison system were trained in MI during 2002-2003. An assessment tool of MI skills developed at the University of Michigan, the I-Pass, is used to certify MI counselors. The program requires that counselors continue to receive peer feedback on their MI skills. An internet program based on MI is being developed to help reduce the stress of correctional officers. MI has been described as the most widely used program in the Swedish justice system and is used as a stand-alone treatment for short-stays and as a strategy used in other lengthier programs. Preliminary outcome research with pre-posttreatment measures has been positive. Some of these measures involve attitudes toward drug use, alcohol use, perceived self-efficacy, internal versus external motivation, and perceived priority of actual change (Arkowitz et al., 2008).

4.8   Schema Therapy and Cognitive Distortions

Many people believe sexual offenders use excuses to justify their behavior and overcome their inhibitions; it is assumed that these excuses increase the likelihood that offenders will commit harmful acts, and therapists try to eliminate clients' use of language that includes justifications and excuses. However, sex offender excuses occur after the crime. Some have argued that excuses and justifications do occur before the crime and thus contribute to offending, but this is unclear. An alternative model of cognitive distortions that has implications for treatment is that faulty information processing is at work in most sexual offenses, and this faulty information processing is due to dysfunctional schemas (Geer, Estupinan, & Manguno-Mire, 2000; Mann & Shingler, 2006).

A schema is defined as a mental structure that guides and filters information processing. Schemas may also include rules, attitudes, self-verbalizations, beliefs, or assumptions (Mann & Shingler, 2006). The contents of a schema can have important themes such as power, respect, suspiciousness, and revenge. The contents of a schema may not be readily available to consciousness. Schema contents may arise from early life experiences when the person is trying to make sense out of what is happening and there is no rational explanation readily available, such as with early child abuse or parental abandonment. Some writers have used other terms interchangeably with schemas, such as scripts and implicit theory (Ward and Keenan, 1999).

Three prominent dysfunctional schemas have been identified in the literature for sex offenders. Hostile masculinity is one schema prominent in sexually coercive males. Malamuth, Heavy, and Linz (1993) argue that date rapists display hostile masculinity and sexual promiscuity early in life. Hostile masculinity without sexual promiscuity leads to nonsexual aggression against women. A second prominent schema with sex offenders is suspiciousness. Malamuth and Brown (1994) set up an experiment with a video of a man making sexual advances toward a woman and the woman responding in one of four ways: friendly, seductive, assertively rejecting, or hostile. The aggressive males interpreted these video scenarios in a way that portrayed suspiciousness. That is, they tended to see women as game-playing and deceptive people. The greater the level of aggressiveness reported in the male's background, the greater his level of suspiciousness. A third prominent schema is sexual entitlement. In a study of incest offenders compared to nonoffending males and male batterers, Hanson, Gizzarelli and Scott (1994) found that sex offenders more frequently report sexual entitlement beliefs, responding positively to items such as "A person should have sex whenever it is needed" and "Women should oblige men's sexual needs." Beck (1999) identified seven schemas related to nonsexual violence: (1) Authorities are controlling and punitive; (2) Spouses are deceitful; (3) Outsiders are hostile; (4) Nobody can be trusted; (5) I need to fight back; (6) Physical force gets respect; and (7) If you do not get even people will walk over you. Mann and Shingler (2006) suggests that these seven can be combined into a "hostile world" schema.

Life maps or life histories can be used as therapeutic tools to help identify dysfunctional schemas in the offenders' lives. The life map exercise has the offender chart significant life experiences and identify life's high points and low points while attempting to identify accompanying thoughts and emotions. When completed, the life maps are presented in groups with opportunities for the therapist and group members to make comments or ask questions. These maps can help a client understand the patterns of his dysfunctional thinking. Mann and Shingler (2006) give the example of a person being bullied at school who develops revenge-oriented thinking as a result of this experience. Later, when a partner is unfaithful, the offender reports experiencing revenge-oriented thinking. This exercise helps the offender recognize dysfunctional schemas and how they endure over time.

Another exercise is to have group members give examples that illustrate when a particular schema has been active, along with the self-talk and par-

A new way of thinking about cognitive distortions in terms of faulty information processing and schemas is needed.

Life histories or life maps can help identify dysfunctional schemas.

ticular cognitions that go along with the schema. For example, if an offender identifies that entitlement is a particular dysfunctional schema, then he could give examples of when this schema became prominent and how it could relate to his sex offending. This exercise can also be helpful in identifying situations that trigger the schema, which is an important step in schema-management (Mann & Shingler, 2006).

It is unlikely that dysfunctional schemas can be significantly changed during a short-term therapy program. Young (1990) defined schemas as "extremely stable and enduring themes that develop during childhood and are elaborated on throughout an individual's lifetime" (p. 9). In therapy, clients are taught to gain skill in recognizing when their dysfunctional schemas are operating, and they learn to challenge their schemas. Mann and Shingler (2006) describe a four-stage process during therapy: (1) Explain the concept of schema; (2) Learn to recognize when schemas are in operation; (3) Learn techniques for managing schema-related cognition; and (4) Role-play schema management in ambiguous or threatening situations. Mann and Shingle (2006) describe a rose-colored glasses exercise that may help clients recognize schemas. In this exercise, clients are encouraged to speculate on what "seeing the world through rose-colored glasses" actually means. Then, the clients are encouraged to consider their own schemas as spectacles through which they view the world. When wearing these spectacles, different situations are perceived in different ways.

The primary tool for helping clients to manage schemas is schema-focused therapy (Padesky 1994; Young, 1990). It is critical that the therapist be vigilant in maintaining a good therapeutic alliance with the clients because sex offenders have difficulties with authority figures as they struggle to articulate emotions and learn self-talk (Marshall, 1993). Occasions will arise during treatment where the client's dysfunctional schemas will become prominent and the therapist needs to be vigilant to identify these occasions, and use them in a supportive fashion to help the client recognize what is happening. A goal of cognitive therapy is to get the client to consider that his beliefs are hypotheses to be tested and not absolute truths. Some exercises suggested by Mann and Shingler (2006) include: (1) Considering the advantages and disadvantages of holding dysfunctional schemas; (2) Thinking about the consequences of schemas in the past and possible future consequences if clients continue to process information in this way; (3) Collecting evidence for and against their schema-related beliefs.

Role-plays can be used to help clients learn to challenge their dysfunctional schemas and develop alternative self-talk. The therapist or group member role-plays a client who has a dysfunctional schema operating. Ambiguous situations that would be negative to everyone (e.g., a spouse leaving) should be selected. Role-plays should be challenging but not so difficult that the client cannot have a positive result with active coaching by the therapist and intervention if the client gets stuck.

Marshall et al. (2006) identify different targets of treatment and then describe treatment strategies to address each of these targets. This description can be used to assess different strategies and tools for both individual and group treatment. Treatment should be organized around specific goals for the clients.

Role-playing can help clients learn to challenge their dysfunctional schemas and develop alternative self-talk.

Identifying targets of treatment and then structuring treatment to address those targets is a practical approach.

4.9   Targets of Treatment

4.9.1   Self-Esteem

Low self-esteem is especially prominent in sex-offenders and should be a key treatment target. Marshall, Anderson, and Champagne (1997) reviewed the literature and found low self-esteem in child molesters and rapists compared to other types of offenders. Fernandez and Marshall (2003) found low self-esteem to be problematic with rapists. Campbell and Lavallee (1993) found that individuals with low self-esteem react more strongly to negative feedback from their environment. It has also been found that people with variable, reactive self-esteem are especially likely to exhibit aggressive and violent behavior (Bushman & Baumeister, 1998). Some therapists believe focusing on self-esteem for offenders who are psychopathic is counterindicated. This position ignores the research that shows that most sex offenders are not psychopathic and the fact that low self-esteem is common among sex offenders. In addition, this position oversimplifies the research on dynamic indicators of risk for sexual re-offending and ignores the important mediating influence of self-esteem on emotional regulation and criminogenic needs of sexually violent men (Laws, 2008).

Clients with low self-esteem do not believe that change is possible. Miller (1983) found that belief in their capacity to change enhances the participation and motivation of clients, and there is evidence that group cohesion leads to enhanced self-esteem with both sex offenders and nonsex offenders (Beech & Fordham, 1997). Thornton, Beech, and Marshall (2004) found that low pretreatment self-esteem scores predicted postrelease failure as accurately as actuarial risk measures. Interestingly, Fernandez, Anderson, and Marshall (1999) found few cognitive distortions in offenders with adequate self-esteem, but high levels of cognitive distortion in those with low self-esteem.

> **Pretreatment self-esteem scores predict postrelease failure as accurately as actuarial risk measures.**

Several strategies can enhance offender self-esteem. An important initial emphasis in treatment is to help the client recognize the difference between himself and his behaviors. In this regard, the therapist can insist that offenders not refer to themselves as sex offenders, but rather as people who have committed sex offenses. In the California Sex Offender Treatment Program, those with sex offenses are referred to as "individuals." This emphasis addresses the shame that is a key impediment to change (Proeve & Howells, 2005).

Another strategy is to work with clients to help them identify and enhance pleasurable activities in their daily lives. The therapist can help clients to identify reinforcing social interactions and to intentionally increase the range and frequency of these pleasurable social interactions. Another strategy is to work to enhance positive self-statements made by the clients. It is useful to have each group member or individual client write on pocket-size cards eight to ten positive statements about themselves. The client is instructed to read those statements at least three times each day while involved in a pleasurable social activity (Marshall et al., 2006).

Targeting self-esteem is important because low self-esteem has been shown to be prevalent with sex offenders, and also because several treatment-relevant characteristics are often present with low-self esteem individuals. These include expectancy to fail at novel tasks, reluctance to commit to change, hesitancy to try new behaviors, failure to practice when learning new skills, becoming discouraged when trying to change, readily giving up, resisting efforts of help, excessive cognitive distortions, low empathy, low social skills, consistent emotional distress, episodic negative affect, overreactive to negative feedback, and poor self-concept (Baumeister, 1993; Marshall et al., 2006). Hanson and Harris (2000) have documented that acute negative emotional states precipitate re-offenses, and therefore it is important for therapists to enhance the self-esteem of sex offenders.

> **Reluctance to commit to change, failure to practice new skills, becoming discouraged, and resisting efforts to help are associated with low self-esteem.**

4.9.2   Acceptance of Responsibility

Acceptance of responsibility is a second important target of treatment (Marshall et al., 2006), and Barbaree (1991) has documented the high levels of denial and minimization among sex offenders. Fifty-four percent (54%) of rapists and 66% of child molesters are described as categorically denying committing their offense, and 98% of all offenders either deny or minimize their offense in some way.

In treatment, the expression of minimizations, denials, and rationalizations are used to challenge the client's cognitive distortions (Mann & Shingler, 2006). Disclosure is used to focus initially on acceptance of responsibility. Hanson and Bussiere (1998) examined the relationship between denial and later re-offending. No relationship was found between any aspect of denial and later re-offending, and therefore exhaustive recounting of all offenses is not thought to be productive and may jeopardize the relationship with the therapist. Marshall et al. (2006) suggests that therapists highlight only two offenses that are typical of others committed by the offender to encourage disclosure. Clients are encouraged early in treatment to disclose regarding these two typical offenses and are reinforced for initial disclosure. They are told that disclosure takes courage. They are also told that this is the first effort and that more detailed disclosure will be required. At the next disclosure session, police reports and victim statements are shared with the client. The therapist emphasizes that the goal of disclosure is to help the client live a more satisfying and offense-free life, and therefore the stress of these sessions is important. Throughout treatment, the client may have to come back to his offenses and disclose more completely. Whenever the clients express distorted perceptions or offense-supportive attitudes, the therapist challenges these distortions in a supportive but firm way and takes every opportunity to identify those instances in which clients try to escape responsibility.

Efforts to minimize or deny the offense or the harm caused may reflect negative scripts or schemas. For example, the negative schema of shame is quite powerful in preventing honest disclosure and acceptance of responsibility. Therefore, forcing the client to agree to all the details in victim statements or police reports may result in compliance but not lead to positive behavior change. Minimization and denial remain a focus of treatment from the beginning. Efforts at disclosure, even if premature and incomplete, are reinforced and negative schemas that prevent accurate disclosure continue to be exampled and addressed (Mann & Shingler, 2006). Cognitive distortions may become more prominent when the client is stressed. Because of this, the therapist works with group members and the client to help each client understand the scripts or schemas that give rise to these cognitive distortions (Mann & Shingler, 2006; Young, 1990).

Efforts to minimize or deny the offense or the harm caused may reflect negative scripts or schemas.

Clients who do not accept the victim's report as legitimate are asked to write out their own account of the offense as if they were the victim. The therapist then reads this out loud to the group in order to emphasize the importance of distortions that may be present. Both the therapist and the group members provide feedback to the client. To facilitate more adequate disclosure, the client is then asked to rewrite this description and, if possible, it is read again by the therapist in a later session with feedback from the group members and the therapist. It is re-read until the disclosure is adequate (Marshall et al., 2006).

4.9.3   Pathways to Offending

Therapists can help clients identify and recognize environmental triggers that lead to them seek out victims. These triggers include relationship conflicts, perception of rejection, financial or work-related stress, boredom, various mood states, emotional loneliness, feeling humiliated, anger, and intoxication (Marshall et al., 2003). Some of these feelings can trigger offense-related fantasies and early offense-specific chain behaviors. Exercises and work on self-disclosure help the clients identify these emotional triggers.

The autobiography or life history exercise can help uncover specific background factors that may be precursors to sex offending. Marshall et al. (2006) have clients write out their life histories, including important relationships, health, education, work, leisure, and events that clients think are important. Clients are encouraged to write or type the life history or autobiography so that the therapist can read it in a group session. For clients who are illiterate or have a low IQ, a scribe the client trusts and who understands the exercise can help the client write the life history. If the life history is too long for the therapist to read, then a synopsis is read. Feedback is provided by the therapist and the other members of the group, and the client may be asked to revise and redo with this feedback in mind. The purpose of this important exercise is to help the therapist and client come to understand personal schema and background factors that may contribute to offending behavior and to generate a hypothesis about what should be emphasized in treatment.

A second important exercise is to have the client come up with a coping plan in which background factors are identified and alternative coping strategies, both behavioral and cognitive, are paired with background factors. The therapist emphasizes that these background factors can be controlled and their influence reduced. A list of the background factors that have been influential in the client's offending behavior is generated with alternative coping strategies. This list is discussed in group and feedback is provided. Flexibility in utilizing coping strategies is an overall objective of treatment. Clients are encouraged to come up with "backup plans" if the first coping strategy does not work with a particular background factor (Marshall et al., 2006).

4.9.4   Victim Empathy

Another target of treatment for sexually coercive males is victim empathy (Pithers, 1999). The first step of empathy training is getting the client to accurately identify and label the emotions within themselves, in others, and in particular their victims (Daniels, 2005). Marshall et al. (2006) describe an exercise to assist with this goal. All group members are asked to describe a particularly emotionally upsetting experience they can recall. They are encouraged to describe this experience as emotionally as they can. Each group member is then encouraged to identify the emotion expressed by the target group member. Then, in turn, each group member is to identify a different emotion expressed by the target group member and describe an emotion that they felt when the emotional story was told.

The victim empathy deficit with sex offenders is primarily toward their victims rather than a generalized empathy deficit.

Research suggests that the victim empathy deficit with sex offenders is primarily toward their victims and may not be a generalized empathy deficit. Barbaree (1990) describes a case that illustrates this narrow empathy deficit with victims. The sexual arousal of a sadist was assessed with phallometric testing while exposed to descriptions of consenting sex, rape, and nonsexual physical abuse of three different women, including his ex-wife, a female friend who supported him, and a current female partner. He expressed strong hostility toward his ex-wife, substantially less hostility toward his friend, and affectionate feelings toward his current partner. When his current partner was the subject in the different scenarios of coercive sex, the sadist showed strong sexual arousal to consenting sex but no arousal with rape. When his friend was the subject, he showed somewhat diminished sexual arousal and almost equal responses to the rape and consenting scenes. When his ex-wife was the subject, he showed no arousal to consenting sex, significant arousal to rape, and full erections to scenes describing her being nonsexually assaulted. Barbaree concluded that empathy deficits are specific to victims and cognitive distortions may allow offenders to avoid shame.

Marshall et al. (2006) suggests a three-stage process in group therapy to help achieve more victim empathy. In the first stage, a group discussion helps the clients identify short-term and long-term results of sexual assault for victims. In the second stage, the offender is directed to think about the consequences for their victim. Again, if the offender has many victims, then have them focus on one victim that may be typical of their other victims. They are to consider each of the consequences generated from the group discussion in stage one and how the consequence would apply to their victim, the victim's family, and their own family. As part of this stage they are also asked to think about and express in group how these consequences would apply if someone they loved were the victim, such as a daughter, wife, or supportive partner and, if abused, how the abuse would make them feel. Marshall et al. (2006) believe this exercise is especially salient and emotional for those with sadistic tendencies.

A final stage of victim empathy training involves having the client write two hypothetical letters. The first letter is a letter from the victim to the offender in which the victim describes his or her anger and distress as a result of the assault. The second letter is from the offender to the victim. In this letter the offender takes full responsibility and communicates the violation of trust, and acknowledges the hurt and harm done to the other person's life. Also, in this letter the offender describes what he is doing in treatment to assure that he will not do this to other people. Marshall et al. (2006) stress that these letters must be emotional rather than intellectual. These hypothetical letters are intended to improve offender recognition of the victim's distress that is not discounted by cognitive distortions. These letters are not mailed or used outside of treatment; instead, they are read in group feedback is provided by the therapist and group members.

Of all the targets of treatment described by Marshall et al. (2006), perhaps victim empathy training has the least empirical support. Intuitively, it does make sense that empathy toward victims can inhibit sexual aggression (Webster et al., 2005). There is some evidence that a tape of a male being raped does seem to have a positive impact on rape myth attitudes in college males (Schewe & O'Donohue, 1996).

4.9.5 Social Skills

According to Marshall et al. (2006), there is an emerging consensus that specific skill deficits associated with impairment in intimacy, attachments, and loneliness should be addressed in treatment. During all sessions, the therapist works with clients to develop communication skills associated with assertiveness, anxiety, and anger. If a client expresses anxiety, anger, or displays social deficits in group, the therapist takes the opportunity to model and promote more adaptive behaviors. Not participating or one-word responses are not permitted, and each client is encouraged to participate in every discussion. If a person gets upset in group, the expression of this anger and hostility is accepted and the source of these feelings is explored with the opportunity to practice good coping skills in a role-play situation. Of course, if the client becomes too hostile and disruptive, he is asked to leave and is referred for anger management training. Also, role plays can be used to help clients develop assertion skills.

> **Specific skill deficits associated with impairment in intimacy, attachments, and loneliness should be addressed in the treatment of sex offenders.**

4.9.6 Healthy Attachment

Therapists can stress the benefits associated with achieving genuine intimacy such as better physical and mental health, greater sexual satisfaction, and overall higher levels of life-satisfaction. Then, adult attachment style names formulated by Bartholomew and Horowitz (1991) can be presented to the group and group members can be encouraged to identify their typical attachment style. These styles are: (1) *Secure*—characterized by the perspective of both positive self and positive others, comfort with intimacy, seeking mutual reciprocity and high intimacy; (2) *Preoccupied*—negative self, positive others, seeking constant approval of others, meeting affection and security needs through sex, overtly dependent on relationships; (3) *Fearful*—negative self, negative others, desiring intimacy, mistrusting of others, fearing closeness, rejection, keeping partner at a distance to avoid rejection/hurt; and (4), *Dismissive*—positive self, negative others, seeing no value in closeness, autonomous, minimal disclosure, blaming, hostile. Clients are helped in this exercise by having them describe important relationships and their feelings and behaviors in these relationships (Marshall et. al, 2006).

The therapist then encourages the client to develop skills of intimacy and adult attachment (Marshall et al., 2006). These discussions include origins of attachment styles, such as early childhood experiences with parents, or early teen and adult experiences, effective communication, jealousy, compatibility, and living without a partner. When stressed, dysfunctional schemas or irrational beliefs about themselves and others may emerge that negatively affects clients' efforts at intimacy. Compatibility with a partner is stressed rather than selection of a sexual partner simply because of appearance. Clients are discouraged from entering relationships too quickly, solely to avoid being alone, before compatibility is assessed. Partners must share a reasonable number of interests and have mutual goals that are enjoyable and satisfying. This usually means that age appropriate partners be considered. The distinction between unfounded jealousy and well-founded jealousy is discussed. If the client is in a current relationship, then clients are encouraged to write out the positive and negative aspects of this relationship and these are discussed in group and suggestions are made for positive changes. Finally, the pros and cons of living alone are discussed. Some of the advantages may include learning how to be self-sufficient, an opportunity to grow in different ways and learn by going to school or traveling, and other ways to grow.

Sex offenders have dysfunctional attachment styles (Smallbone, 2005; Smallbone & Dadds, 1998). Some theorists have even outlined a model that categorizes the victims of sexually aggressive men based on dysfunctional attachment styles (Ward, Hudson, Marshall and Siegert, 1995).

Loneliness is the reciprocal of attachment/intimacy (Marshall et al., 2006) and it predicts aggressive behavior (Check, Perlman, & Malamuth, 1985). Clients explore the fact that sometimes people can experience loneliness even when they are in a relationship. Therapists focus on intimacy and attachment to help the client develop skills to reduce loneliness, enhance intimacy, and secure adult attachment skills. Written exercises that encourage the client to explore his past communications and/or current relationships are used to examine how these communications can be improved.

4.9.7   Emotional Regulation

Learning effective coping skills to help with mood management is an important focus of treatment. Serran and Marshall (2005) have established a connection between coping and mood and argue that it is bi-directional. That is, inadequate coping leads to unstable mood and unstable mood leads to inadequate coping. We know that different types of sex offenders (i.e., child-molesters) have a tendency to use avoidance-focused coping and sex as a coping strategy (Cortoni & Marshall, 2001). Marshall et al. (2006) describe a group process in which a basic scheme of styles of coping is presented. These styles include problem-focused coping, emotion-focused coping, and avoidance-focused coping (Endler & Parker, 1999). Through group discussion clients learn how to identify different coping styles, and they are asked to identify situations in the past when they used good coping skills and situations when they did not. They are assisted in identifying the emotional and behavioral antecedents for good coping and inadequate coping. This assistance is through open-ended exploratory questions. Using specific examples, the therapist and group members make suggestions about how the client could have coped better, and role-plays are used to provide opportunities for the client to practice and rehearse good coping skills. Marshall et al. (2006) suggest that therapists should clarify that clients will not always be supported or reinforced for successful coping.

Hanson and Harris (2000) have shown that emotional dysregulation is a significant risk factor for sex crime re-offending and should be a focus of treatment. There are many different types of stressors in an offender's life that can contribute to emotional dysregulation. These include long hours of work with little leisure, abuse of alcohol and drugs, mismanagement of finances, and sometimes catering to the needs of others and feeling that personal needs have been sacrificed. These stressors may lead to an attitude of entitlement (Hanson et al., 1994). An important task in treatment is to help the client generate good coping strategies with concrete suggestions about how to get help in particular situations, such as seeking out counseling, seeking support from friends and family, or making an appointment to see a psychiatrist. A critical element in the appraisal process when a person is stressed is optimism about whether he or she will be able to cope successfully (Lazarus & Folkman, 1984). This optimistic appraisal determines the adequacy of the coping process. Helping clients utilize task-focused coping and providing opportunities to practice coping skills in treatment helps clients become more confident that they can cope effectively without resorting to sex offending.

Emotional dysregulation is directly linked with low self-esteem (Baumeister, 1993). Therefore, treatment that enhances self-esteem should help clients utilize good coping skills. Recognizing and modulating emotional responsiveness is also a part of empathy training, and thus multiple targets of treatment address emotional dysregulation. It is important to encourage group members to practice emotional regulation and coping skills outside of sessions and to bring back their successes and challenges so that they can be described and discussed in group (Marshall et al., 2006).

Emotional dysregulation has been directly linked to low self-esteem; treatment that enhances self-esteem will help clients utilize good coping skills.

4.9.8   Deviant Sexual Fantasies

Deviant sexual interests or fantasies increase the likelihood of sex offending (Quinsey et al., 1998), and are therefore an important target of treatment. However, the assessment of deviant sexual interests and fantasies poses significant problems. Typically, four different strategies have been used to assess deviant interests. These are: (1) Self-report; (2) Phallometric assessments (Murphy and Barbaree, 1994); (3) Psychological tests (e.g., the Multiphasic Sex Inventory) (Nichols and Molinda, 1984); and (4) Attention time while observing deviant stimuli (e.g., the Abel Screen) (Abel, 1995). However, the nature of deviant sexual fantasies makes them difficult to accurately assess and treat. For example, intoxication with alcohol changes the nature of sexual fantasies in normal males (Barbaree, Marshall, Yates, and Lightfoot, 1983). Also, when a woman makes a normal man angry, he is more likely to have rape fantasies than when he is not angry (Yates, Barbaree, & Marshall, 1984).

Conflict and mood have a direct impact on the presence and nature of sexual deviant fantasies (Looman, 1999).

Behavior modification and medications are the two major strategies that have been used to treat deviant sexual interest/fantasies. Marshall et al. (2006) outlined helpful criteria that can be used before deciding to implement behavior modification with incarcerated offenders; these same criteria are appropriate with decisions for referrals for medications. These criteria include: (1) A sexual history that reveals high rates of deviant acts that are persistent over time; (2) Phallometric evaluations that demonstrate significant arousal to deviant stimuli; (3) Self-reports of persistent deviant sexual fantasies or sexual arousal in response to staff or persons seen in the media; (4) Institutional records that show attempted sexual assault against staff or other inmates.

There are several important precautions to bear in mind before commencing treatment. The major concern is that there is little research on the long-term effectiveness of these strategies to reduce recidivism for sex offenders. However, there is some research that demonstrates that deviant sexual fantasies are significantly influenced by treatment strategies that do not focus specifically on deviant sexual fantasies. Marshall (1997b) reports a study of 12 nonfamilial child molesters who had low self-esteem ratings and deviant sexual fantasies as measured with phallometric ratings. A full treatment program was designed to improve self-esteem. Change scores from pre- to posttreatment were calculated on self-esteem and these change scores correlated highly with associated reduction in sexual deviant fantasies. Marshall (1997b) stressed that there was no behavioral treatment provided for deviant sexual fantasies, but the levels of sexual deviant fantasies dropped to normal levels when self-esteem improved. Marshall (1997) described these results as "powerful" if replicated. He further concluded that these results call into question the "wisdom of exposing sexual offenders to pornographic-like images or descriptions of women and children in phallometric evaluations .... and employing masturbatory reconditioning" (p. 94). Marshall (1997b) quotes other leaders in the behavioral treatment of sex offenders (e.g., Gene Abel and Bill Pithers) who have observed reductions in deviant sexual fantasies in response to the successful implementation of other components of comprehensive programs. Thus, the need to focus on deviant fantasies as a target of treatment is now coming into question.

Another review of behavioral strategies to alter sexual arousal has encouraged a cautious approach to the treatment of sexual offenders (Dougher, 1995). In particular, Dougher argues that classical conditioning guidelines should be rigorously followed in order to help insure success. Because some of the procedures involve counterconditioning procedures in which sexually deviant stimuli are paired with unpleasant stimuli, strict adherence to ethical and legal guidelines is essential. It is important to have informed consent with a clear rationale for why these strategies are used, as well as criteria for when they should be discontinued. In light of these implementation issues, the possible negative influence on the therapeutic alliance, and the fact that good pharmacotherapy alternatives are available, these procedures should be used with caution.

Recent research has questioned the wisdom of exposing offenders to deviant images or descriptions in the treatment of deviant sexual fantasies. In contrast, enhanced self-esteem is directly related to decreases in deviant sexual fantasies.

4.9.8.1 Behavior Modification

Marshall et al. (2006) use four different behavioral techniques to address deviant sexual fantasies. The first is foul odor aversion. Marshall contends that this procedure is effective immediately and the positive results of decreased fantasies are enduring. Sustainable results are often achieved in as few as 6 sessions of pairings. The process involves pairing strong foul odors (e.g., valeric acid, mercapto-ethanol, or rancid meat) with deviant images/thoughts. The procedure and practice details are discussed in individual sessions with the client. Because the procedure may impede the development of a good client-therapist relationship and the practical problems associated with the treatment, Marshall recommends using this procedure as a last resort – even though it is believed to be one of the most effective treatments for sexual offenders.

Ammonia aversion is a behavioral procedure closely related to foul odor. Clients who report deviant sexual thoughts/fantasies that are intrusive and task-interfering are asked to carry a small vial of smelling salts of ammonia. Whenever unwanted sexual thoughts occur, the client is instructed to rapidly inhale the ammonia. Marshall et al. (2006) contend that because the effects of ammonia are mediated by the body's pain system instead of the olfactory system, the exposure removes sexually deviant thoughts and allows clients to substitute nonsexual thoughts.

A third behavioral strategy is covert association or covert sensitization. Marshall et al. (2006) prefer the former name since the effectiveness of the procedure is primarily due to the pairing of the sequence of the deviant chain of behavior/thoughts and thoughts with the actual consequences of behavior rather than with an external negative stimulus. The therapist helps the client identify several behavioral/emotion/thought chains of prior offenses and reconstruct his fantasies. It is ideal to use five or six sequences, which are then broken down into six to eight steps. Each step is written on a pocket size card with its consequences on the back of the card. The consequences need to be realistic. The client is instructed to read the sequences and their consequences three times each day. Checks are made in individual counseling to make sure this practice is followed with diligence. In the early stages of treatment, the sequences are read through completely before the consequences are read. During later weeks of practice, the client progressively moves the reading of the consequences to an earlier interruption of reading the sequences. After four to six weeks, the consequences should be read when the client is contemplating initiating the offense.

Masturbatory reconditioning is a fourth behavioral strategy. The objective with this procedure is to increase sexual responsiveness to appropriate stimuli and decrease sexual responsiveness to deviant images. The client is first encouraged to identify an age appropriate person with whom they might have consensual sex. The client can pick a male or female depending on his sexual preference. Erotic images can be used at the beginning with some men who have difficulties generating attraction to internal images, but in general, the use of pornographic images is discouraged. The client is encouraged to shape his fantasies about their appropriate partners and consenting sex (Marshall et al., 2006).

The client is given permission to become aroused using deviant fantasies when he begins masturbation, and then, when aroused, switch to the more appropriate image in his fantasies. If arousal subsides, he resumes using whatever images are necessary to become aroused, and then once again switches to the appropriate image. The client is instructed to repeat this sequence every time he masturbates (Marshall et al., 2006). The goal is to have appropriate images excite the client; this assumes that the practice will decrease the valence of the inappropriate fantasies. Marshall emphasizes that there is no danger associated with this treatment because the inappropriate fantasies are already present and highly arousing. If clients object to using masturbation as a part of their treatment, other behavioral strategies or medication can be used.

Satiation training is another strategy that can be used as an adjunct treatment to masturbatory reconditioning. Immediately after orgasm from masturbation, the client can verbally rehearse deviant sexual fantasies while in a refractory period of sexual nonresponsiveness. The refractory period occurs within two minutes of orgasm. This pairing of deviant sexual fantasies with sexual non-reward extinguishes the attractiveness of the deviant sexual fantasies (Marshall et al., 2006). The generation of deviant sexual fantasies during a period of non-reward decreases the frequency and potency of the fantasies. The repetition of the deviant fantasies for approximately 10 minutes after orgasm leads to extinction of the arousal value of the fantasies.

Marshall et al. (2006) recommend combining these behavioral strategies. For example, verbal satiation and covert association are combined, and if the person continues to report intrusive sexual deviant fantasies and thoughts, then masturbatory reconditioning and olfactory aversion are used. The argument for masturbatory reconditioning is that this strategy attempts to help the client develop sexual arousal to appropriate fantasies and thoughts. Guidance and checks are provided in individual sessions. Clients are asked to keep daily logs of the frequency and intensity of their fantasies, including both deviant and appropriate thoughts.

4.9.8.2 Pharmacological Interventions

Medications can be an important part in the treatment of sexual offenders. Bradford (2000, 2006) has advocated the use of medications with all "hands-on" sex offenders. Two classes of medication that have been used effectively in the treatment of sex offenders are selective serotonin reuptake inhibitors (SSRIs) and antiandrogens. SSRIs are used when the frequency of sexual activity is high (i.e., 11 or more times per week, even though intrusive fantasies may not be reported). Antiandrogens are used to reduce the circulating testosterone levels in the blood. These medications can help clients who engage in compulsive sexual behavior. With medication treatment, clients are asked to keep a log of their sexual fantasies and frequency of masturbation (Marshall et. al, 2006).

> Treatment of deviant sexual interests with either serotonin reuptake inhibitors (SSRIs) or antiandrogens is effective.

Research has shown that SSRIs and other drugs that block dopamine can be effective in the treatment of paraphilias, nonparphilic hypersexuality, and compulsive sexual behavior (Adi et al., 2002). SSRIs can have positive effects on sexual behavior similar to the antiandrogens, without some of the negative side effects. Decreased serotonin levels in the brain have been associated with increases in sex drive, whereas increased levels have been associated with reduction in sex drive in experimental animals. SSRIs are most often used for the treatment of depression, obsessive-compulsive disorder, panic disorder, and other conditions, but the sexual side effects are helpful in the treatment of paraphilia.

Some sexual deviant behavior is associated with possible underlying neurobiological abnormalities and compulsive disorders. The literature has documented a relationship between sexual behavior problems and frontal lobe lesions. Also, sexually deviant behavior has been associated with temporal lobe epilepsy, post-encephalitic syndromes, septal lesions, Tourette disorder, frontal lobe lesions, cerebral tumors in various parts of the brain, bilateral temporal lobe lesions, and multiple sclerosis (Kafka, 2008). This research suggests paraphilias may be appropriately catalogued with the obsessive-compulsive spectrum disorders.

Another form of treatment uses hormonal agents like estrogen to reduce sexual drive. Medroxyprogesterone (MPA) has been the most important hormonal agent used in the United States, and this hormone clearly results in a reduction in testosterone. Research documents successful reduction in sex drive, sexual fantasy, and sexual activity when patients are given MPA. Significant side-effects include potential diabetes mellitus, headaches, weight gain, deep vein thrombosis, hot flashes, nausea, and vomiting (Kafka, 2008). A final group of drugs used to treat sexual offenders are antiangrogens, such as cyproterone (CPA), which have their primary influence on the body's androgen receptors. These drugs block intracellular testosterone uptake and the intracellular metabolism of androgen. Sexual behavior decreases because of the reduction of plasma testosterone; this includes erections, masturbation, sexual intercourse, and deviant sexual behavior. These drugs also have been used in the treatment of prostate cancer and have the side effect of complete reduction or elimination of testosterone, effectively resulting in pharmacological "castration." The side effects can be similar to MPA along with the possibility of liver dysfunction and adrenal suppression. Long-term use can lead to osteoporosis.

Bradford and Fedoroff (2006) have proposed a six level algorithm for the pharmacological treatment of paraphilias. Treatment recommended in each of these stages include: (1) Cognitive-behavioral treatment of all paraphilias of any severity; (2) Pharmacological treatment would start with SSRIs with mild paraphilias; (3) If SSRIs are not effective in 4–6 weeks at adequate dosages, then a small dose of an antiandrogen is added and this is recommended for mild and moderate paraphilias; (4) Full antiandrogen treatment or hormonal treatment given orally in moderate and some severe cases; (5) Full antiandrogen treatment or hormonal treatment given intramuscularly for severe paraphilias; and (6) Complete androgen suppression and sex-drive suppression by cyproterone intramuscularly for severe cases.

To aide in applying this algorithm, Bradford and Fedoroff (2006) composed a severity rating to be used in conjunction with a DSM diagnosis of paraphilia. This classification system has four levels: (1) *Mild*—brief paraphilic fantasy only, including all "hands-off" paraphilias such as exhibitionism, voyeurism, and fetishism; (2) *Moderate*—would include "hands-on" paraphilias such as pedophilià, provided the number of victims was low, and the level of intrusive sexual behavior is limited to fondling; (3) *Severe*—includes "hands-on" paraphilias with a large number of victims and evidence of intrusive sexual behavior beyond fondling; and (4) *Catastrophic*—includes cases in which sexual sadism is the defining feature.

4.9.9   Self-Management Plans

A final target of treatment is the development of self-management plans. Rather than focusing on plans to avoid re-offending, which is an avoidance

Therapists should encourage clients to practice skills that enhance self-efficacy.

goal, plans can be constructed with clients that focus on building more pro-social lives that will enable them to achieve their life goals. Developing more effective goals that are clearly and discretely articulated in their life plans will reduce their risk of re-offending. Therapy focuses on building positive and rewarding life goals and this leads to increased optimism about the possibility for change (Marshall et al., 2006).

It is crucial for therapists to help clients gain a sense of hope (Fernandez, 2006). Hope is a primary factor leading to positive therapeutic change, and therapists should use every opportunity in therapy to have clients practice skills that enhance self-efficacy. Clients low in hope will give up readily when blocked in their pursuit of goals (Snyder, 2000). Beech and Fordham (1997) found that one of the most crucial elements leading to positive change in group therapy for sex offenders was instilling hope in the clients.

In group therapy, therapists help clients build their own life plans. The Good Lives Model (Ward, 2002; Ward & Stewart, 2003) is used to guide group discussion. Primary goods are identified that can be individualized by group members in their life plans. These include life-healthy/optimal functioning in-cluding sexual satisfaction, knowledge, excellence in work and play, autonomy and self-directedness, inner peace, relatedness, spirituality, happiness, and creativity. Their life plans allow the clients to bring together all that they have learned in therapy, including identifying cognitive distortions and dysfunc-tional schemas, learning skills to enhance self-esteem, learning to control their emotions, and improving interpersonal and communication skills to help them achieve their goals. For example, some therapy time is used to help clients think about strategies to create good leisure activities.

It can be helpful to have clients identify risk situations that threaten their life plans and strategies to avoid and/or cope with those situations. These risks can be related to the research of Hanson and Harris (2000) on dynamic risk factors. Each client is asked to list the sequence of risks associated with their offenses, and the therapist emphasizes that there can be new risk sequences and so clients needs to be aware of novel ways they may have to cope. The therapist provides different scenarios of novel risks and asks the client to gen-erate several coping strategies to these new risks. This exercise helps clients generalize the coping skills they have developed (Marshall et al., 2006).

It is important that relapse plans be created, but they should not be so detailed that the person becomes overwhelmed with avoidance goals. Approach goals are necessary if the person is to be motivated to change.

Marshall et al. (2006) list several reasons why traditional approaches that involve creating detailed relapse prevention plans may not be useful. Such plans tend to be very detailed and focus primarily on avoidance goals that are less likely to be implemented than approach goals such as those listed by Ward (2002). In addition, some relapse prevention plans contain so many situations to avoid that the client may become overwhelmed. Not all possible risks can be listed or identified, and having a canned list of situations or emotions to avoid may give the client the false sense that they are completely safe from sex of-fending. Because of these reasons, therapists should list risky situations while emphasizing that not all risks can be anticipated and therefore the client's new skills need to generalize to novel circumstances and risk situations.

Clients are helped to generate lists of indicators or warning signs that signal that the client may be at risk for offending. Two lists are generated by the client (Marshall et al., 2006). One list contains signs that the client would recognize and another list includes indicators to others that the client is at risk. These lists are based on the client's past history and situations the client believes may be risks for him. These lists can then be presented in group and client coping responses to each risk situation can prompt group discussion. It is important to help the client identify more than one coping response to each risk situation to promote generalization of coping skills to novel situations. These lists of risky situations or warning signs are refined and become part of the client's record and are shared with other providers or probation and parole officers working with the client and with members of the client's support group.

Because support groups and supportive individuals are so important to the client's progress in the community (Wilson & Picheca, 2005), the client is asked to make two lists of support people who will be important. The first list includes professionals that the client will utilize or see, such as a counselor, minister, parole officer, etc. The second list is composed of friends and family members (Marshall et al., 2006).

Finally, each client is asked to generate a plan for transition back to the community that is realistic and that provides the client with the necessary supports to help assure success. The plan must be specific enough to include details about where to live, employment or preparations for employment, education, how to make friends, leisure activities, and interaction with companions. The therapist and the group help to review how realistic these plans are, and they help the client revise as necessary. The therapist works with the client to begin making the necessary preliminary contacts to begin implementation of the plan while still in group or in the institution (Marshall et al., 2006).

4.10   A Special Population—Individuals with Developmental Disabilities

One special population of sex offenders that needs to be discussed are those with developmental disabilities (DD). Because of their cognitive limitations, special consideration needs to be given to identify those treatment strategies most likely to be effective. These individuals usually are those who meet DSM IV criteria for borderline or mild mental retardation. Some researchers have indicated higher prevalence rates for sex offending for this population (Day, 1994). However, Haaven and Coleman (2000) have reviewed the literature and have not found this population to be overrepresented among sex offenders.

Individuals with developmental disabilities are not overrepresented among the sexually violent, as is commonly believed.

The typical relapse prevention modal is not appropriate for the DD population because of significant differences in individuals with DD compared to other sex offenders. These differences involve learning capacity, self-esteem, and coping skills. Different strategies are needed for persons with developmental disabilities. For example, offense chains would be difficult for DD persons to understand. Because of their feelings of inadequacy and fears about being labeled "dumb," these individuals often are overly sensitive to criticism and resistant to change. They have greater deficits in social skills and thus greater problems with emotional controls because of the difficulties they encounter in getting their needs met (Haaven & Coleman, 2000).

Haaven and Coleman (2000) recommend an approach to self-management for DD persons that does not require that they understand the offense sequence

A treatment approach can be used with individuals with DD that does not require an understanding of their offense cycle, but is positive and focuses on the "New Me" versus the "Old Me."

and all the cognitions and emotions involved. This approach focuses on positive goals rather than avoidance goals. The framework would have the DD persons identify the "New Me" and the "Old Me." Characteristics and goals of the New Me are clarified and contrasted with those of the Old Me. Clients may picture the New Me as powerful, wise, good to others, etc. Corresponding principles and behaviors that go with these ideal New Me characteristics can include, "I stand up for what's right," "I can wait," etc. Treatment then focuses on set-ups (situations) that keep them from having a good life and achieving the New Me, or situations that put them in danger of re-offending. Treatment also focuses on what-to-dos. The strategies and skills that the DD person identifies and learns to achieve the New Me include self-management skills, interpersonal skills, problem solving skills, and help seeking skills.

A group format is the best treatment approach for DD persons. However, shorter and more frequent groups are appropriate (e.g., 30 minutes, four times per week). The group environment must be a safe, warm, respectful, and humane environment. Some strategies that can be helpful include the use of animals (Coleman, 1997), with use of collages, pictures, videotaping, and role-plays where every effort is made to celebrate the New Me identity change. Even though group therapy is the preferred treatment modality, sometimes DD persons are not ready for the exposure in group and some individual therapy may be needed before the person joins a group. Haaven and Coleman (2000) suggest that group time can be focused with the use of action-oriented techniques such as drama therapy, mindfulness techniques, and refreshment breaks. The groups should be small (no more than 8 clients), and the group leader will have to be more directive than with non-DD clients. DD persons have learned to respect caregivers and to discount their peers, and so more direction from the therapist is essential. Therapists will need to frequently confront the denial of their DD clients who have committed sexual offenses.

It is essential that the therapy process be success-oriented and that all role-plays, exercises, and similar activities end in success. When discussing the What-to-Dos and the different strategies to achieve the New Me, one coping skill is chosen as the Primary New Me focus throughout therapy. Adapting regular strategies to meet the learning capabilities of those with DD is essential. For example, DD persons can draw pictures of key events in their lives and these pictures can serve as their autobiographies. It can be helpful to organize these pictures in terms of before, during, and after the crime. Using a camcorder to record role-plays illustrating how to escape risky situations and achieve the New Me may be helpful. Having board games where members draw cards and then role play New Me behaviors with the therapist can be a useful strategy in light of the ineffectiveness of regular didactic instruction from the therapist (Haaven & Coleman, 2000).

DD persons are especially handicapped in identifying their emotions in high risk emotional situations. It is sometimes useful to focus on physical signs of emotional reactions, such as sexual arousal, blushing, or the hand tremors that accompany anxiety. It may be productive to focus on clients' emotional reactions in specific concrete situations, such as being in the presence of a child, alcohol, pornography, etc. During transition to a less restrictive environment, group therapy can help clients identify high risk situations and practice New Me skills through role-plays (Haaven & Coleman, 2000).

4.11   Best Practices in Treatment of Sexually Violent Persons

A useful way to summarize the most recent thinking about best practices in sex offender treatment is to highlight some of the key points in the *Practice Standards and Guidelines of the Association for the Treatment of Sexual Abusers* (ATSA) (2005). The *Practice Standards and Guidelines* list some principles and assumptions based on research and recognized good clinical practice:

1. Most individuals who sexually offend will benefit from effective treatment interventions.
2. Inadequate, inappropriate, or unethical treatment is harmful to the client.
3. Management of risk factors is a life-long endeavor.
4. Internal motivation of the client is important for treatment compliance, but external motivation, such as court mandates, may be necessary for some abusers.
5. A court order, prosecution, or other legal directive for specialized sex offender treatment may be important requirements for effective treatment and management.
6. A specialized evaluation of treatment need and supervision is important before releasing abusers to the community.
7. Effective management of sexually coercive men requires working collaboratively with other therapists, advocates, community organizations, probation and parole, child welfare, and others involved with monitoring clients and preventing abuse in the community.

Given these basic assumptions, the *Practice Standards and Guidelines* provide directions for working with sexually abusive males. Structured cognitive-behavioral and skills-oriented approaches that specifically target criminogenic needs have been shown to be the most effective. The *Standards and Guidelines* also recognize that prescribed medications can be a valuable adjunctive therapy. Of course, the distinction between cognitive-behavioral and insight-oriented therapies is not always clear in actual practice. For example, schema therapy as a way to identify and change cognitive distortions seems to be important. However, schema therapy combines elements of cognitive-behavioral therapy and insight-oriented therapy (Young, 1990). The targeting of treatment on criminogenic needs comports with the extensive work of Andrews and Bonta (2006) regarding effective treatment of general criminal behavior. The *Standards and Guidelines* operationalize criminogenic needs by equating them with the dynamic risk factors identified in the literature for sexually abusive males, i.e., those characteristics of offenders that can be targeted for therapeutic change. Some of these are listed in the *Standards and Guidelines* and include: access to potential victims, insufficient or inappropriate employment, inappropriate living circumstances, inappropriate use of leisure time, substance misuse, intimacy deficits, emotional management deficits, sexual preoccupation, deviant sexual interests, deviant sexual arousal, attitudes supportive of offending, antisocial lifestyle and associates, and lack of cooperation with supervision.

Best practices in sex offender treatment focuses on "criminogenic" needs.

The *Standards and Guidelines* recommend that the intensity of treatment be matched to the client's risk. They go further to indicate that providing an

Current standards of care indicate that you can overtreat in a way that may negatively affect a client's risk.

Current standards of care indicate that the modality of treatment should match the client's needs.

inappropriate level of intensity of treatment "may negatively affect a client's risk" (p. 19). This was a concern in the SOTEP program and may be a concern with many offenders civilly committed for long periods under the sexual violent predator laws. Clearly more research is needed to address this problem (Marshall & Yates, 2005).

Another important standard is that clinicians provide treatment in a way so that clients will be receptive and responsive. Thus, client characteristics must guide how treatment is provided. Some of these characteristics include IQ, learning style, personality, culture, mental and physical disabilities, and motivation. The treatment that is effective focuses on the client's strengths and builds on those strengths in treatment planning. The *Standards and Guidelines* recognize that treatment can be provided in different modes, such as individual, family, and group therapy. Rather than advocating for group therapy over other therapy modalities, the *Standards and Guidelines* indicate that group treatment is most common, but then they recommend using whatever modality matches the client's needs and circumstances.

4.12 Cultural Considerations in Sex Offender Treatment

It is important when providing sex offender treatment to be aware of different cultural values that may shape the schemas, cognitive distortions, effective reward structures, and self-efficacy of clients. Sex offender treatment strategies must incorporate different cultural values to be effective with different groups of clients. It is also important to assess the individual's personal identification as well as family history and ethnic background.

Unique cultural factors should be considered when providing treatment to Native Americans who are sex offenders. These include lack of trust in the dominant culture, emotional numbing, and the high prevalence of depression.

The different treatment needs of Asian Americans, Hispanics, and Native Americans illustrate the importance of incorporating different cultural values in sex offender treatment. For example, there can be significant cultural differences in the worldviews of Native American clients based on their tribal identification (Ertz, 1997). The Native American culture has been shaped by a history of trauma and violence. This violence can take the form of racial prejudice, violence from within the family, poverty, and systems of dependence. As a result, emotional numbing, alcoholism, and impaired social relations, including inadequate parenting skills, sometimes predominate. A lack of trust of those in the dominant culture may be present, which has a direct impact on the therapist-client relationship. It is also important for the clinician to be vigilant in considering the importance of mood regulation with Native Americans because some data indicate that there are higher prevalence rates of depression and bipolar disorder among Native Americans (Ertz, 1997).

As the result of these cultural differences, special considerations are necessary when treating Native Americans. Whenever possible, traditional tribal or family beliefs should be integrated into treatment. Major cultural differences can exist in socialization patterns that are directly pertinent to goal setting and developing strategies to achieve goals. These socialization differences can involve accepting emotional support, expressing and allowing others to express emotions, and acceptance of ownership for both behaviors and emotions. If these differences are not addressed, bonding with the therapist may not occur and the client may not become engaged in treatment. An especially important cultural difference with Native Americans is found in behavioral management. Erik Erickson (1950) observed more than 50 years ago that antecedents, such as positive role modals, are more important for Native Americans, whereas consequences are more prominent in traditional change modals.

Cultural considerations are also important when helping a client develop an internal locus of control. For example, Ertz (1997) points out that some Native American tribes believe in sharing of shame among family and tribal groups, and this is very different from the traditional view of individual responsibility. These cultural considerations must be considered by the therapist in working with Native American sex offenders.

When working with Hispanic sex offenders, clinicians needs to be aware of different ways of thinking and feeling associated with cultural differences from Anglo-Americans. Carrasco and Garza-Louis (1997) have reported survey findings showing clear cultural differences among Hispanics, Mexican Americans, African Americans, and Anglo Americans on characteristics that would influence sex offending and responsiveness to treatment. These cultural characteristics are associated with the concepts of *macho* and *machismo*. It is important to understand that these authors define "macho" and "machismo" from the perspective of the Hispanic culture, and these definitions are different from the popular vernacular. *Macho* is a good quality, and it is associated with true pride, honoring women, the male being authoritarian, but respectful, protective, faithful, and responsible. In contrast, *machismo* is associated with false pride, arrogance, dishonoring women, disrespectful and authoritarian attitudes, infidelity, and irresponsible behaviors. It is obvious that attitudes associated with *machismo* are related to sexual coercion (e.g., arrogance, abuse of power in the family, double standards, degradation of women, promiscuity, and alcoholism). Hispanic offenders do hold stronger *machista* or chauvinistic attitudes than other sex offenders, even though they also hold traditional values about the family. Hispanic sex offenders often confuse or distort the differences between *macho* and *machismo*.

An example of this distortion is found in the concept of filial obedience. In traditional Mexican culture, the father receives unquestioned obedience from his children. In a healthy Hispanic family, this unquestioned obedience occurs in the context of love/responsibility, which is a part of the self-concept of *macho*. The macho father not only expects unquestioned obedience, but views this obedience as a privilege that is earned through his love, responsibility, and protection. However, this *macho* concept is confused with *machismo* in the specific case of sex offending with stepdaughters, and a large proportion of Hispanic offenders have molested their stepdaughters. Hispanic offenders of stepdaughters tend to refer to them as *entenadas* (i.e., foster children) rather than *hijastras* (stepdaughters). This distancing of the relationship allows the Hispanic sex offender to take advantage of the filial obedience in their culture without the love and responsibility and facilitates child sexual abuse of stepdaughters. Treatment can focus on the distortion of the responsibility of *macho* and the client's confusion about the attitudes of *macho* and *machismo* (Carrasco & Garza-Louis, 1997), and therapists can help clients replace *machismo* attitudes and behavior with truly *macho* attitudes and behaviors.

Important concepts in the Hispanic culture that can influence understanding and treating sexually violent persons include the confusion between *macho* and *machismo*, the unquestioned authority of the father and mother-love.

Another concept that can sometimes be used in treatment is the importance in Hispanic culture of mother-love. Even thought the mother does not have the authority of the father, she is granted unquestioned love from her children and husband. The special status of the mother can be used in therapy to help the client accept that his culture does not condone his behaviors because it is an affront to the special status of women and mothers (Carrasco & Garza-Louis, 1997).

When treating Asian Americans, it is important to know whether their peer group is prosocial or antisocial. A protective factor that can be included in treatment is losing face with their peers.

Understanding cultural differences also can play an important role in implementing effective treatment for Asian Americans. Some have argued that current conceptualizations of sexual coercion are inadequate when considering Asian Americans (Hall, Teten, & Sue, 2003). The distinction between the individualistic cultural orientation of European American men versus the collectivist cultural orientation of Asian Americans can have significant implications for understanding sexual coercive behavior in Asian Americans and in planning treatment. Hall and associates argue that across studies, approximately 30% of Asian Americans acknowledge sexually coercive behavior, which is not significantly different from other ethnic groups. European American men's sexual coercion has been presented as individually determined attitudes, beliefs and behaviors associated with hostility toward women, early sexual promiscuity, rigid male roles, acceptance of male-female conflict, etc. However, Asian American men's sexual coercion appears to be a combination of these attitudes and beliefs and cultural considerations. Misogynous beliefs (i.e., hatred of women) are found in both European Americans and Asian Americans; however, an additional protective factor for Asian American men against sexual coercive behavior is the fear of losing social standing. Hall, Teten and Sue (2003) conducted a structured equation modeling analysis and found that for European American men there was a clear path of dominance and hostility toward women that led to sexually coercive behavior, but for Asian Americans there was an additional path to coercive sexual behavior that included loss of face as a protective factor. This protective factor did not influence the behavior of European Americans.

Treatment with Asian American sex offenders should focus on peer group influences. Hall et al. (2003) have suggested that whether the concern of losing face is a protective factor or a risk factor could be determined by whether the reference group of influence is prosocial or antisocial. Thus, cognitions, emotions, and behaviors in treatment that are associated with losing face in the relationship of the client with their peer group become more important than with other cultures that are more individualist.

4.13   Summary and Conclusions

An overarching theme of this book has been the complexity of sexually violent behavior. Not all sexually coercive and violent individuals are the same nor do they progress on the same pathway to offending behavior. This book has reviewed the research literature and examined hundreds of studies that involve community and noncriminal samples of criminal offenders. Each area of research contributes unique perspectives that enhance our overall understanding of sexually coercive behavior. It is clear that a multivariate approach to understanding sexually coercive behavior is most appropriate, and simple explanations of either distal or proximal causes do not adequately describe the complexity of these harmful behaviors.

Another theme of this book is that most sexually violent and coercive individuals *can* be successfully treated. Treatment should be evidenced-based. Treatment should adequately address the internal and external motivation of sexually coercive individuals. Treatment that is evidence-based includes both approach and avoidance goals. A positive therapeutic alliance is essential for treatment gains, regardless of what treatment strategies are adopted, and therefore therapist training and supervision are important.

Much work has been done on identifying the needs of sexually coercive individuals that should be addressed in treatment, including targeting high-risk clients with more intense treatment. Targets of treatment should include self-esteem, acceptance of responsibility, pathways of offending/relapse prevention, victim empathy, social skills, healthy attachment and intimacy, coping skills, emotional regulation, and goal planning. This list of targets of treatment is not exhaustive.

The research literature is expanding rapidly in this important arena of treatment. We do know that most sexually violent individuals can be helped with evidenced-based treatment, but we also know that some individuals in treatment are made worse, and we still have much to learn about why this occurs and how we can be more effective in our treatment efforts.

5

Case Vignettes

The following case illustrates the influence of male stereotypical role attitudes and hypersexuality in a young, intelligent college student.

Case #1 (Joe)

A prominent family court attorney brought her 17-year-old son to see a local psychologist. The mother reported that her son's grades had dramatically decreased over the course of the last year. She also reported that last year her son had gotten into trouble with juvenile officials because he was a passenger in a "joy riding" incident accompanying a friend who had stolen a car. The mother also mentioned that her son would stay out some weeknights and weekends beyond his curfew and would not tell her where he had been. The mother was divorced and there was a great deal of hostility between the mother and her ex-husband, primarily over money. The father was a house construction builder in the local town. When interviewed, the son reported that he was no longer interested in school. He worked at a local golf course and was spending more time with friends. He acknowledged that he liked to drink beer and that every weekend he and his friends would have a party. He also acknowledged that two or three nights a week he would also drink a few beers. He said that he did not have a steady girlfriend but enjoyed being with girls. He acknowledged that he had sexual intercourse with more than 40 college women, and sometimes he would have sex with "three or four" different women during a week. Birth control was an important concern for him, but he believed that it was ultimately the girl's responsibility to make sure she would not get pregnant. In describing his promiscuous lifestyle, he indicated that "most of the time they come after me." He added that they liked him to be assertive and even aggressive, and many times sexual intercourse would occur when he and his partner were drinking alcohol. He began having sex with girls when he was 14 years old, but in the last year, the frequency had dramatically increased and was consuming more of his energy and time.

The following case illustrates the influence of several factors in a brutal rape, including an acquaintance rape, cognitive distortions, and anger, and hostility toward women.

Case #2 (John)

John is a 32-year-old African American who had a previous history of assault, but within a very conflicted relationship with his ex-girlfriend, with whom he had a two-year-old son. John had been terminated from his job as a fork-lift operator after approximately 4 years of employment because of frequent absences. John had been diagnosed with depression and had been taking antide-pressant medications inconsistently after an inpatient involuntary hospital stay subsequent to a fight with his ex-girlfriend and threats of homicide and suicide approximately six months ago. Recently, John had been fighting frequently with his ex-girlfriend over his lack of dependability in baby-sitting for his two-year-old son, and his ex-girlfriend's decision to limit his time with his son. John's mother had been ill, and recently died; John attempted to borrow money from his ex-girlfriend to take a bus to his mother's funeral. His ex-girlfriend refused, but somehow John got enough money to go to his mother's funeral. When he got back into town from the funeral he called his ex-girlfriend for a ride from the bus station, but she indicated that she had to go to work. John then called his ex-girlfriend's sister who came and picked him up. They then returned to her apartment where she was going to change before going to work. John had been drinking beer before she picked him up from the bus station. He violently raped his ex-girlfriend's sister, forcing both anal and vaginal inter-course several times and forcing her to perform oral sex. When interviewed, John indicated that he had dated the sister in the past and she was "always in love with me." The police reports of the victim indicated that she persistently asked him to stop and that there was significant injury to the victim.

The following case illustrates the "grooming" and planning involved in some sexual violent cases.

Case #3 (MM)

MM is a 28-year-old African American male who was under pretrial evalu-ation after being charged with seven counts of sodomy. The victims were a 14-year-old boy and his 16-year-old brother. MM met the first victim at a video game mall where he provided the victim with tokens and afterward they went to a movie, and then to MM's house. The next weekend the victim came to the offender's house. After becoming intoxicated with beer, the victim was asked to take off his clothes; the two began fondling each other and the offender had anal sex with the victim. The following weekend MM bought the victim approximately $350 worth of clothes and a pair of shoes, and again had anal sex with him. The offender went to the victim's house and asked his brother if he wanted to come over to his house as well. The second victim had noticed that his brother had the new clothes. The offender again provided beer to the second victim. He also made up a rule for a monopoly game that if the victim landed on one of his properties and could not pay, then he would have to "down a whole can of beer." The victim further added, "The next thing I realized I was down on the floor in the computer room and he was touching my penis and making me touch his. Then he took off my clothes and made me suck his penis and then he started to have intercourse with me. I was telling him to stop because it hurt. He took me to a room with a waterbed and we had intercourse. I was tightening up my butt muscles so he couldn't do anything. I told him to quit because it hurt. He stopped and said, 'I almost came, but you're trying to make me stop.'" The offender bought both victims more clothes.

MM was born when his mother was 15 years old. They lived with his grandmother while his mother tried to finish high school. The father was not involved. The mother reports that a friend from church sexually abused MM, and her brother's friend also abused him. The mother reports that she was not a good mother, and that she often screamed at MM, and left him by himself after the age of ten. She suffered from chronic depression and has had 28 surgeries in the last 16 years. MM did graduate from high school and attended college, but dropped out. He has worked several jobs including being a car salesman. He reports that he drinks six or seven beers a day and uses marijuana about once a month. He has suffered from depression, and periodically has received professional treatment. He served 5 years in prison for a previous charge of sodomy. The psychologist who examined him believed that he was malingering mental illness and low intelligence.

The following is a case of child sex abuse where early parental abuse and sexual abuse may have been distal contributing factors.

Case #4 (JC)

JC is a 40-year-old divorced white male who was accused of sexual assault of a female child. The victim's mother came to the local police and reported that her live-in boyfriend had raped her 6-year-old daughter. The mother had known JC for approximately 10 years, and he had taken care of the victim and her brother while she recovered from surgery. He had lived with the mother and her children for approximately 6 months. After watching a TV show on sexual abuse one night, the daughter reported to the mother and the police that she had had sex with JC. The victim was given a medical evaluation and the results reported that, "hymen changes are consistent with repetitive, chronic, manipulation and possible penetration with a foreign object." The victim told the examiners that JC had put "his privates into my privates." She indicated that JC had taken her into her mother's bedroom and had taken off her clothes and his clothes and laid on top of her. She also reported that he put her on top of him and moved her up and down. He also had her bite his fingers so she would not scream. She also described JC fondling her genitalia and placing his penis in her mouth. During an interview with a psychologist, JC indicated that he had begun having thoughts of having sex with the victim after she had told him that she had had sexual relations. The night before the offense, JC began drinking beer after a year of sobriety. He described spreading the victim's labia and looking at her and concluding that she had not had sex before because she was "very small." He then reported that he pulled up her underwear because, "It hit me that what I was doing was wrong."

JC's early family life was very disrupted, and his parents had been abusive to each other and to him. He indicated that a 16-year-old boy anally raped him when he was 13. He was placed in foster care, but ran away and spent a good deal of time in juvenile treatment facilities. He was married at the age of 23 for six months, and this marriage ended when he became involved with another woman. He was in the Marine Corps for a short time and was discharged because his personality was incompatible with military service. At the time of the offense, he was a self-employed electrician. He has a significant history of alcohol abuse, which had started before the age of 10. At the time of his arrest, he reportedly was drinking a case of beer per day and using marijuana daily. His IQ testing indicated a full-scale IQ of 89. He had two prior offenses of disorderly conduct 20 years previously and an assault charge for hitting his son.

6

Further Reading

1. Marshall, W. L., Marshall, L. E., Serran, G. A., & Fernandez, Y. M. (2006). *Treating sexual offenders: An integrated approach*. New York: Routledge, Taylor & Francis Group.
   These authors provide a good description of the treatment targets and strategies for the program that presently has the best evidence of effectiveness. Some of the treatment targets and strategies presented in the present work are described in this book.
2. Hanson, R. K., Bourgon, G., Helmus, L., & Hodgson, S. (2009). *A meta-analysis of the effectiveness of treatment for sexual offenders: Risk, need, and responsivity*. Public Safety Canada. Her Majesty the Queen in Right of Canada, Cat. No.: PS3-1/2009-2E-PDF.
   This is important research on what factors predict positive treatment outcomes. This article presents dynamic risk indicators and how these indicators can be viewed according to the most prominent theory of treatment effectiveness with corrections populations.
3. Ward, T., & Beech, A. R. (2008). An integrated theory of sexual offending. In R. D. Laws & W. T. O'Donohue (Eds.), *Sexual deviance: Theory, assessment, and treatment* (pp. 21–36). New York: Guilford Press.
   This article brings together all of the most recent research and theorizing about sex offenders into an integrated theory. This theory provides a rationale for treatment strategies with different types of offenders.
4. Fernandez, Y. (Ed.) (2002). *In their shoes: Examining the issue of empathy and its place in the treatment of offenders*. Oklahoma City: Wood 'N' Barnes Publishing & Distribution.
   One of the most important targets of treatment is victim empathy. This book presents research, theory and strategies for addressing victim empathy.

7

References

Abbey, A., Clinton, A. M., McAuslan, P., Zawacki, T., & Buck, P. O. (2002). Alcohol-induced rapes: Are they more violent? *Psychology of Women Quarterly, 26,* 99–109.

Abbey, A., McAuslan, P., & Ross, L. T. (1998). Sexual assault perpetration by college men: The role of alcohol, misperception of sexual intent and sexual beliefs and experiences. *Journal of Social and Clinical Psychology, 17,* 167–195.

Abel, G. G. (1995). *New technology: The Abel Assessment for Interest in Paraphilias.* Atlanta, GA: Abel Screening Inc.

Abel, G. G., Becker, J. V., Mittelman, M. S., Cunningham-Rathner, J., Rouleau, J. L., & Murphy, W. D. (1987). Self-reported sex crimes of nonincarcerated paraphiliacs. *Journal of Interpersonal Violence, 2,* 3–25.

Abel, G. G., Huffman, J., Warberg, B., & Holland, C. L. (1998). Visual reaction time and plethysmography as measures of sexual interest in child molesters. *Sexual Abuse: A Journal of Research and Treatment, 10,* 81–95.

Abel, G. G., Jordan, A. D., Hand, C. G., Holland, L. A., & Phipps, A. (2001). Classification modals of child molesters utilizing the Abel assessment for sexual interest. *Child Abuse & Neglect, 25,* 703–718.

Ackerman, S. J., & Hilsonroth, M. J. (2003). A review of therapist characteristics and techniques positively impacting on the therapeutic alliance. *Clinical Psychology Review, 23,* 1–33.

Adi, Y., Ashcroft, D., Browne, K., Beech, A., Fry-Smith, A., & Hyde, C. (2002). Clinical effectiveness and cost-consequences of selective serotonin reuptake inhibitors in the treatment of sex offenders. *Health Technology Assessment, 6,* 1–65.

Allen, M., D'Alessio, D., & Brezgel, K. (1995). Exposure to pornography and acceptance of rape myths. *Journal of Communication, 45,* 5–26.

Almeyer, S., Keinsasser, D., Stoner, J., & Retzlaff, P. (2003). Psychopathology of incarcerated sex offenders. *Journal of Personality Disorders, 17,* 306–318.

American Psychiatric Association. (2000). *Diagnostic and statistical manual of mental disorders* (4th ed., text revision). Washington, DC: Author.

Amrhein, P. C., Miller, W. R., Yahne, C. E., Palmer, M., & Fulcher, L. (2003). Client commitment language during motivational interviewing predicts drug use outcome. *Journal of Consulting and Clinical Psychology, 71,* 862–878.

Andrews, D. A., & Bonta, J. L. (2001). *The Level of Service Inventory-revised: User's manual.* Toronto:Multi-Health Systems, Inc.

Andrews, D. A., & Bonta, J. (2006). *The psychology of criminal conduct* (4th ed.). Cincinnati, OH: Anderson Publishing.

Annis, J. D., & Chan, D. (1983). The differential treatment model: Empirical evidence from a personality typology of adult offenders. *Criminal Justice and Behavior, 10,* 159–173.

Arkowitz, H., & Miller, W. R. (2008). Learning, applying, and extending motivational interviewing. In H. Arkowitz, H. A. Westra, W. R. Miller, & S. Rollnick (Eds.), *Motivational interviewing in the treatment of psychological problems* (pp. 1–25). New York: Guilford Press.

Arkowitz, H., & Westra, H. (2004). Integrating motivational interviewing and cognitive behavioral therapy in the treatment of depression and anxiety. *Journal of Cognitive Psychotherapy, 18,* 337–350.

Ashby, J. D., Ford, D. H., Gueney, B. G., & Guerney, L. F. (1957). Effects on clients of a reflective and leading type of psychotherapy. *Psychological Monographs, 453, 71.*

Association for the Treatment of Sexual Abusers (2005). *Practice standards and guidelines for members of the Association for the Treatment of Sexual Abusers.* Beaverton, Oregon: Author.

Atwood, J. D., & Gagnon, J. (1987). Masturbatory behavior in college youth. *Journal of Sex Education and Therapy, 13,* 35–42.

Bachelor, A. (1988). How clients perceive therapist empathy: A content analysis of "received" empathy. *Psychotherapy, 25,* 227–240.

Barbaree, H. E. (1990). Stimulus control of sexual arousal: Its role in sexual assault. In W. L. Marshall, D. R. Laws, & H. E. Barbaree (Eds.), *Handbook of sexual assault: Issues, theories, and treatment of the offender* (pp. 115–142). New York: Plenum Press.

Barbaree, H. E. (1991). Denial and minimization among sex offenders: Assessment and treatment outcome. *Forum on Corrections Research, 3,* 300–333.

Barbaree, H. E., Marshall, W. L., Yates, E., Lightfoot, L. O. (1983). Alcohol intoxication and deviant sexual arousal in male social drinkers. *Behavioral Research and Therapy, 21,* 365–373.

Bard, L. A., Carter, D. L., Cerce, D. D., Knight, R. A., Rosenberg, R., & Schneider, B. (1987). A descriptive study of rapists and child molesters: Developmental, clinical, and criminal characteristics. *Behavioral Sciences and the Law, 5,* 203–220.

Bargh, J. A., Raymond, P., Pryor, J. B., & Strack, F. (1995). Attractiveness of the underling: An automatic power-sex association and its consequences for sexual harassment and aggression. *Journal of Personality and Social Psychology, 68,* 768–781.

Barkman, M., & Shapiro, D. A. (1986). Counselor verbal response modes and experienced empathy. *Journal of Counseling Psychology, 33,* 3–10.

Bartholomew, K., & Horowitz, L. (1991). Attachment styles among young adults: A test of a four-category model. *Journal of Personality and Social Psychology, 61,* 226–244.

Baumeister, R. F. (Ed.) (1993). *Self-esteem: The puzzle of low self-regard.* New York: Plenum Press.

Beck, A. T. (1999). *Prisoners of hate: The cognitive basis of anger, hostility and violence.* New York: Harper Collins.

Becker, J. V., & Stein, R. M. (1991). Is sexual erotica associated with sexual deviance in adolescent males? *International Journal of Law and Psychiatry, 14,* 85–95.

Beech, A. & Fordham, A. S. (1997). Therapeutic climate of sexual offender treatment programs. *Sexual Abuse: A Journal of Research and Treatment, 9,* 219–237.

Beech, A. R., & Hamilton-Giachritsis, C. E. (2005). Relationship between therapeutic climate and treatment outcome in group-based sexual offender treatment programs. *Sexual Abuse: A Journal of Research and Treatment, 17,* 127–140.

Bennice, J., & Resick, P. (2003). Marital rape: History, research, & practice. *Trauma, Violence, & Abuse, 4,* 228–246.

Bergen, R. K., & Bukovec, P. (2006). Men and intimate partner rape: Characteristics of men who sexually abuse their partner. *Journal of Interpersonal Violence, 21,* 1375–1384.

Beutler, L. E., Pollack, S., & Jobe, A. M. (1978). "Acceptance," values and therapeutic change. *Journal of Consulting and Clinical Psychology, 46,* 198–199.

Boer, D. R., Hart, S. D., Kropp, P. R., & Webster, C. D. (1997). *Manual for the Sexual Violence Risk–20: Professional guidelines for assessing risk of sexual violence.* Burnaby, British Columbia, Canada: Mental Health, Law, & Policy Institute, Simon Fraser University.

Borowsky, I. W., Hogan, M., & Ireland, M. (1997). Adolescent sexual aggression: Risk and protective factors. *Pediatrics, 100,* 7.

Bradford, J. M. W. (2000). The treatment of sexual deviation using a pharmacological approach. *Journal of Sex Research, 3,* 248–257.

Bradford, J. M. W. (2001). The neurobiology, neuropharmacology, and pharmacological treatment of paraphilias and compulsive sexual behavior. *Canadian Journal of Psychiatry, 46,* 26–33.

Bradford, J. M. W., & Fedoroff, P. (2006). The pharmacological treatment of the juvenile sex offender. In H. E. Barbaree & W. L. Marshall (Eds.), *The juvenile sex offender* (2nd ed.) (pp. 358–382). New York: Guilford Press.

Branaman, T. F., & Gallagher, S. N. (2005). Polygraph testing in sex offender treatment: A review and limitations. *American Journal of Forensic Psychology, 23,* 45–64.

Brecklin, L. R., & Forde, D. R. (2001). A meta-analysis of rape education program. *Violence and Victims, 16,* 303–321.

Brecklin, L. R., & Ullman, S. E. (2002). The roles of victim and offender alcohol use in sexual assaults: Results from the National Violence Against Women Survey. *Journal of Studies on Alcohol, 63,* 57–63.

Brehm, S. S., & Brehm, J. W. (1981). *Psychological reactance: A theory of freedom and control.* New York: Academic Press.

Brittain, R. P. (1970). The sadistic murderer. *Medicine, Science and the Law, 10,* 198–207.

Burgess, A. W., & Holmstrom, L. L. (1974). Rape trauma syndrome. *American Journal of Psychiatry, 131,* 981–986.

Burk, L. R., & Burkhart, B. R. (2003). Disorganized attachment as a diathesis for sexual deviance: Development experience and the motivation for sexual offending. *Aggression and Violence, 8,* 487–511.

Burke, B., Arkowitz, H., & Menchola, M. (2003). The efficacy of motivational interviewing: A meta-analysis of controlled clinical trials. *Journal of Consulting and Clinical Psychology, 71,* 843–861.

Bushman, B. J., & Baumeister, R. F. (1998). Threatened egotism, narcissism, self-esteem, and direct and displaced aggression: Does self-love or self-hate lead to violence? *Journal of Personality and Social Psychology, 75,* 219–229.

Campbell, J. D., & Lavallee, L. F. (1993). Who am I? The role of self-concept confusion in understanding the behavior of people with low self-esteem. In R. F. Baumeister (Ed.), *Self-esteem: The puzzle of low self-regard* (pp. 3–20). New York: Plenum Press.

Carkhuff, R. R., & Pierce, R. M. (1975). *Trainer's guide: The act of helping.* Amherst, MA: Human Resource Development Press.

Carr, J. L., & VanDeusen, K. M. (2004). Risk factors for male aggression on college campuses. *Journal of Family Violence, 19,* 279–289.

Carrasco, N. & Garza-Louis, D. (1997). Hispanic sex offenders—cultural characteristics and implications for treatment. In B. K. Schwartz & H. R. Cellini (Eds.), *The sex offender: New insights, treatment innovations and legal developments* (Vol. 2) (pp. 13.1–13.8). Kingston, NJ: Civic Research Institute.

Carter, D. L., Prentky, R. A., Knight, R. A., Vanderveer, P. L., & Boucher, R. J. (1987). Use of pornography in the criminal and developmental histories of sexual offenders. *Journal of Interpersonal Violence, 2,* 196–211.

Catalano, S. M. (2005). *Criminal victimization, 2004 (Bureau of Justice Statistics, National Crime Victimization Survey NCJ 210674).* Washington, DC: US Government Printing Office.

Check, J. V. P., Perlman, D., & Malamuth, N. M. (1985). Loneliness and aggressive behavior. *Journal of Social and Personal Relations, 2,* 243–252.

Christensen, K., & Knussman, R. (1987). Androgen levels and components of aggressive behavior in men. *Hormones and Behavior, 21,* 170–180.

Cohen, J. (1969). *Statistical power analysis for the behavioral sciences.* New York: Academic Press.

Coker, A. L., Smith, P. H., McKeown, R. E., & King, M. J. (2000). Frequency and correlates of intimate partner violence by type: Physical, sexual, and psychological battering. *American Journal of Public Health, 90,* 553–559.

Coleman, E. M. (1997). Animal-facilitated sex offender treatment. In B. K. Schwartz & H. R. Cellini (Eds.), *The sex offender: New insights, treatment innovations and legal developments* (Vol. 2) (pp. 21.1–21.11). Kingston, NJ: Civic Research Institute.

Conte, J. R., & Schuerman, J. R. (1987). The effects of sexual abuse on children: A multidimensional view. *Journal of Interpersonal Violence, 2,* 380–390.

Cook , R. F., Fosen, R. H., & Pacht, A. (1971). Pornography and the sex offender: Patterns of previous exposure and arousal effects of pornographic stimuli. *Journal of Applied Psychology, 55,* 503–511.

Cooley, E. J., & LaJoy, R. (1980). Therapeutic relationship and improvements as perceived by clients and therapists. *Journal of Clinical Psychology, 36,* 562–570.

Cormier, W. H., & Cormier, L. S. (1991). *Interviewing strategies for helpers.* Pacific Grove, CA: Brooks/Cole.

Cortoni, F. A., & Marshall, W. L. (2001). Sex as a coping strategy and its relationship to juvenile sexual history and intimacy in sexual offenders. *Sexual Abuse: A Journal of Research and Treatment, 13,* 27–43.

Daniels, M. (2005). The use of role-play to develop victim empathy and relapse prevention. In: B. K. Schwartz & H. R. Cellini (Eds.), *The sex offender: Corrections, treatment, and legal practice* (Vol. 1) (pp. 8.1–8.18). Kingston, NJ: Civic Research Institute.

Davidson, G. C., & Valins, S. (1969). Maintenance of self-attributed and drug-attributed behavior change. *Journal of Personality and Social Psychology, 1,* 25–33.

Davis, K. C., Norris, J. N., George, W. H., Martell, J., & Heiman, J. R. (2006). Men's likelihood of sexual aggression: The influence of alcohol, sexual arousal, and violent pornography. *Aggressive Behavior, 32,* 581–589.

Day, K. (1994). Male mentally handicapped sex offenders. *British Journal of Psychiatry, 165,* 630–639.

De Vogel, V., De Ruiter, C., Van Beck, D., & Mead, G. (2004). Predictive validity of the SVR-20 and Static 99 in a Dutch sample of treated sex offenders. *Law and Human Behavior, 28,* 235–251.

DiClemente, C. C. (1991). Motivational interviewing and the stages of change. In W. R. Miller & S. Rollnick (Eds.), *Motivational interviewing: Preparing people to change addictive behavior* (pp. 191–202). New York: Guilford Press.

Dietz, P. E., Hazelwood, R., & Warren, J. (1990). The sexually sadistic criminal and his offenses. *Bulletin of the American Academy of Psychiatry and the Law, 18,* 163–78.

Divasto, P. V., Kaufman, L. R., Jackson, R., Christy, J., Pearson, S., & Burgett, T. (1984). The prevalence of sexually stressful events among females in the general population. *Archives of Sexual Behavior, 13,* 59–67.

Donnerstein, E., & Berkowitz, L. (1981). Victim reactions in aggressive erotic films as a factor in violence against women. *Journal of Personality and Social Psychology, 41,* 710–724.

Doren, D. M. (2002). *Evaluating sex offenders: A manual for civil commitments and beyond.* Thousand Oaks, CA: Sage Publications.

Dougher, M. (1995). Behavioral techniques to alter sexual arousal. In B. K. Schwartz & H. R. Cellini (Eds.), *The sex offender: Corrections, treatment and legal practice* (Vol. 1) (pp. 15.1–15.8). Kingston, NJ: Civic Research Institute.

Dowden, C., Antonowicz, D., & Andrews, D. A. (2003). The effectiveness of relapse prevention with offenders: A meta-analysis. *International Journal of Offender Therapy and Comparative Criminology, 47,* 516–528.

Drapeau, M. (2005). Research on the processes involved in treating sexual offenders. *Sexual Abuse: A Journal of Research and Treatment, 17,* 117–125.

Dunsieth, N. W., Nelson, E. B., Brusman-Lovins, L. A., Holcomb, J. L., Beckman, D., Welge, J. A., et al. (2004). Psychiatric and legal features of 113 men convicted of sexual offenses. *Journal of Clinical Psychiatry, 65,* 293–300.

Elliott, R., Barker, C. B., Caskey, N., & Pistrang, N. (1982). Differential helpfulness of counselor verbal response modes. *Journal of Counseling Psychology, 29,* 354–361.

Emmons, R. A. (1996). Striving and feeling: Personal goals and subjective well-being. In: P. M. Gollwitzer & J. A. Bargh (Eds.), *The psychology of action: Linking cognition and motivation to behavior* (pp 313–337). New York: Guilford Press.

Endler, N. S., & Parker, J. D. A. (1999). *The coping inventory for stressful situations: Manual* (2nd ed.). Toronto: Multi-Health Systems.

Erickson, E. H. (1950). *Childhood and society.* New York: Norton.

Ertz, D. J. (1997). The American Indian sexual offender. In B. K. Schwartz & H. R. Cellini (Eds.), *The sex offender: New insights, treatment innovations and legal developments* (Vol. 2) (pp. 14.1–14.10). Kingston, NJ: Civic Research Institute.

Fabian, J. M. (2005). The risky business of conducting risk assessments for those already civilly committed as sexually violent predators. *William Mitchell Law Review, 32,* 81–159.

Fago, D. P. (1999). Comorbidity of attention deficit hyperactivity disorder in sexually aggressive children and adolescents. In B. Schwartz (Ed.), *The sex offender: Theoretical advances, treating special populations and legal developments* (Vol. 3) (pp. 16.11–16.15). Kingston, NJ: Civic Research Institute.

Falk, D. R., & Hill, C. E. (1992). Counselor interventions preceding client laughter in brief therapy. *Journal of Counseling Psychology, 39,* 39–45.

Farbring, C. A., & Johnson, W. R. (2008). Motivational interviewing in the correctional system: An attempt to implement motivational interviewing in criminal justice. In H. Arkowitz, H. A. Westra, W. R. Miller & S. Rollnick (Eds.), *Motivational interviewing in the treatment of psychological problems* (pp. 304–323). New York: Guilford Press.

Fernandez, Y. M. (Ed.) (2002). *In their shoes: Examining the issue of empathy and its place in the treatment of offenders.* Oklahoma City: Wood 'N' Barnes Publishing & Distribution.

Fernandez, Y. M. (2006). Focusing on the positive and avoiding the negative in sexual offender treatment. In W. L. Marshall, Y. M. Fernandez, L. E. Marshall, & G. A. Serran (Eds.), *Sexual offender treatment: Controversial issues* (pp. 187–197). Chichester, UK: John Wiley & Sons Ltd.

Fernandez, Y. M., Anderson, D., & Marshall, W. L. (1999). The relationship among empathy, cognitive distortions, and self-esteem in sexual offenders. In B. K. Schwartz (Ed.), *The sex offender: Theoretical advances, treating special populations and legal developments* (Vol. 3) (pp. 4.1–4.12). Kingston, NJ: Civic Research Press Institute.

Fernandez, Y. M., & Marshall, W. L. (2003). Victim empathy, social self-esteem and psychopathy in rapists. *Sexual Abuse: A Journal of Research and Treatment, 15,* 11–26.

Fernandez, Y. M., & Serran, G. (2002). Empathy training for therapists and clients. In Y. M. Fernandez (Ed.), *In their shoes: Examining the issue of empathy and its place in the treatment of offenders* (pp.110–131). Oklahoma City: Wood 'N' Barnes Publishing & Distribution.

Fist, M. B., & Halon, R. L. (2008). Use of DSM paraphilia diagnosis in sexually violent predator commitment cases. *Journal of the American Academy of Psychiatry and the Law, 36,* 443–454.

Fischer, L., & Smith, G. (1999). Statistical adequacy of the Abel Assessment for Interest in Paraphilias. *Sexual Abuse: A Journal of Research and Treatment, 11,* 195–205.

Fisher, W. A., & Barak, A. (1991). Pornography, erotica, and behavior: More questions than answers. *International Journal of Law and Psychiatry, 14,* 65–83.

Foubert, J. D. (2000). The longitudinal effects of a rape-prevention program on fraternity men's attitudes, behavior intent, and behavior. *The Journal of American College Health, 48,* 158–163.

Foubert, J. D. (2005). *The men's program: A peer education guide to rape prevention* (3rd ed.). New York: Taylor & Francis Group.

Frank, J. (1971). Therapeutic factors in psychotherapy. *American Journal of Psychotherapy, 25,* 350–361.

Frank, J. (1974). Therapeutic components of psychotherapy: A 25-year progress report of research. *Journal of Nervous and Mental Disease, 159,* 325–342.

Frieze, I. (1983). Investigating the causes and consequences of marital rape. *Signs: Journal of Women in Culture and Society, 8,* 532–553.

Fuchs, C. Z., & Rehm, L. P. (1977). A self-control behavior therapy program for depression. *Journal of Consulting and Clinical Psychology, 45,* 206–215.

Fuller, F., & Hill, C. E. (1985). Counselor and helper perceptions of counselor intentions in relations to outcome in a single counseling session. *Journal of Counseling Psychology, 32,* 329–338.

Furby, L., Weinrott, M. R., & Blackshaw, L. (1989). Sex offender recidivism: A review. *Psychological Bulletin, 105*, 3–30.

Galli, V., McElroy, S. L., Soutello, C. A., Kizer, D., Raute, N., Keck, P. E., et al. (1999). The psychiatric diagnoses of twenty-two adolescents who have sexually molested other children. *Comprehensive Psychiatry, 40*, 85–87.

Gallagher, C. A., Wilson, D. B., Hirshfield, P., Coggsehell, M. B., & Mackenzie, D. L. (1999). A quantitative review of the effects of sexual offender treatment on sexual offending. *Corrections Management Quarterly, 3*, 19–29.

Garfield, S., & Bergin, A. (Eds.) (1986). *Handbook of psychotherapy and behavior change.* New York: Wiley.

Geer, J. H., Estupinan, L. A., & Manguno-Mire (2000). Empathy, social skills, and other relevant cognitive processes in rapists and child molesters. *Aggression and Violent Behavior, 5*, 99–126.

George, W. H., Stoner, S. A., Norris, J., Lopez, P. A., & Lehman, G. L. (2000). Alcohol expectancies and sexuality: A self-fulfilling prophecy analysis of dyadic perceptions and behavior. *Journal of Studies on Alcohol, 61*, 168–176.

Gidycz, C. A., Warkentin, J. B., & Orchowski, L. M. (2007). Predictors of perpetration of verbal, physical, and sexual violence: A prospective analysis of college men. *Psychology of Men & Masculinity, 8*, 79–94.

Gomes-Schwartz, B. (1978). Effective ingredients in psychology: Prediction of outcome from process variables. *Journal of Consulting and Clinical Psychology, 46*, 1023–1035.

Gratzer, T., & Bradford, M. W. (1995). Offender and offense characteristics of sexual sadists: A comparative study. *Journal of Forensic Sciences, 40*, 450–455.

Greenfield, L. A. (1997). *Sex offenses and offenders: An analysis of data on rape and sexual assault* (US Department of Justice Report NCJ-163392). Washington, DC: US Government Printing Office.

Groth, N., & Gary, T. (1981). Marital rape. *Medical Aspects of Human Sexuality, 15*, 126–131.

Gudjonsson, G. H., & Sigurdsson, J. F. (2000). Differences and similarities between violent offenders and sex offenders. *Child Abuse and Neglect, 24*, 363–372.

Haaven, J. L., & Coleman, E. M. (2000). Treatment of the developmentally disabled sex offender. In D. R. Laws, S. M. Hudson & T. Ward (Eds.), *Remaking relapse prevention with sex offenders: A source-book* (pp. 369–388). Thousand Oaks, CA: Sage Publications.

Hall, G. C. (1995). Sexual offender recidivism revisited: A meta-analysis of recent treatment studies. *Journal of Consulting and Clinical Psychology, 63*, 802–809.

Hall, G. C., Teten, A. L., & Sue, S. (2003). The cultural context of sexual aggression: Asian Americans and European American perpetrators. In R. A. Prentky, E. S. Janjus & M. C. Seto (Eds.), *Sexually coercive behavior: Understanding and management* (pp. 131–143). New York: The New York Academy of Sciences.

Hanson, R. K. (1997). *The development of a brief actuarial risk scale for sexual offense recidivism.* Ottawa, Ontario, Canada: Department of the Solicitor General.

Hanson, R. K., Bourgon, G., Helmus, L., & Hodgson, S. (2009). *A meta-analysis of the effectiveness of treatment for sexual offenders: Risk, need, and responsivity.* Public Safety Canada. Her Majesty the Queen in Right of Canada, Cat. No.: PS3-1/2009-2E-PDF.

Hanson, R. K., & Bussiere, M. T. (1998). Predicting relapse: A meta-analysis of sexual offender recidivism studies. *Journal of Consulting and Clinical Psychology, 66*, 348–362.

Hanson, R. K., Gizzarelli, R., & Scott, H. (1994). The attitudes of incest offenders: Sexual entitlement and acceptance of sex with children. *Criminal Justice and Behavior, 21*, 187–202.

Hanson, R. K., Gordon, A., Harris, A. J. R., Marques, J. K., Murphy, W. D., Quinsey, V. L., et al. (2002). First report of the Collaborative Outcome Data Project on the Effectiveness of Psychological Treatment of Sex Offenders. *Sexual Abuse: A Journal of Research and Treatment, 14*, 169–195.

Hanson, R. K., & Harris, A. J. (2000). Where should we intervene? Dynamic predictors of sexual offense recidivism. *Criminal Justice and Behavior, 27*, 6–35.

Hanson, R. K., Morton, K. E., & Harris, J. R. (2003). Sexual offender recidivism risk: What we know and what we need to know. In R. A. Prentky, E. S. Janus, & M. C. Seto (Eds.), *Sexually coercive behavior: Understanding and management* (pp. 154–166). New York: The New York Academy of Sciences.

Hanson, R. K., & Thornton, D. (2000). Improving risk assessments for sex offenders: A comparison of three actuarial scales. *Law and Human Behavior, 24*, 119–136.

Hare, R. D. (2003). *Hare Psychopathy Checklist-Revised (PCL-R)* (2nd ed.). Toronto, Ontario: Multi-Health Systems, Inc.

Hazelwood, R. R., Dietz, P. E., & Warren, J. I. (1992). The criminal sadist. *FBI Law Enforcement Bulletin, 61*, 12–20.

Henry, F., & McMahon, P. (2000). What survivors of child sexual abuse told us about the people who abuse them. Paper presented at the National Sexual Violence Prevention Conference. Dallas, Tx. Cited in W. L. Marshall, L. E. Marshall, G. A. Serran & Y. M. Fernandez (Eds.) (2006), *Treating sexual offenders: An integrated approach* (p. 2). New York: Routledge, Taylor, & Francis Group.

Henry, N. M., Ward, T., & Hirshberg, M. (2004). Why soldiers rape: An integrated model. *Aggression and Violent Behavior, 9*, 535–562.

Heppner, M. J., Good, G. E., Hillenbrand-Gunn, T. L., Hawkins, A. K., Hacquard, L. L., Nichols, R. K., et al. (1995). Examining sex differences in altering attitudes about rape: A test of the elaboration likelihood model. *Journal of Counseling and Development, 73*, 640–647.

Herman, J. L. (1990). Sex offenders: A feminist perspective. In W. L. Marshal, D. R. Laws, & H. E. Barbaree (Eds.), *Handbook of sexual assault: Issues, theories, and treatment of the offender* (pp. 177–193). New York: Plenum Press.

Hettema, J., Steele, J., & Miller, W. R. (2005). Motivational interviewing. *Annual Review of Clinical Psychology, 1*, 91–111.

Hovath, A. O., & Symonds, B. D. (1991). Relation between working alliance and outcomes in psychotherapy: A meta-analysis. *Journal of Counseling Psychology, 38*, 139–149.

Hoyer, J., Kunst, H., & Schmidt, A. (2001). Social phobia as a comorbid condition in sex offenders with paraphilia or impulse control disorder. *Journal of Nervous and Mental Disease, 189*, 463–470.

Jaffee, D., & Strauss, M. A. (1987). Sexual climate and reported rape: A state-level analysis. *Archives of Sexual Behavior, 16*, 107–123.

Jespersen, A. F., Lalumiere, M. L., & Seto, M. (2009). Sex abuse history among adult sex offenders and non-sex offenders: A meta-analysis. *Child Abuse & Neglect, 33*, 179–192.

Johnson, J. D., Noel, N. E., & Sutter (2000). Alcohol and male acceptance of sexual aggression: the role of perceptual ambiguity. *Journal of Applied Social Psychology, 30*, 1186–1200.

Kafka, M. P. (2003). Sex offending and sexual desire: The clinical and theoretical relevance of hypersexual desire. *International Journal of Offender Therapy and Comparative Criminology, 47*, 439–451.

Kafka, M. P. (2008). Neurobiological processes and comorbidity in sexual deviance. In D. R. Laws & W. T. O'Donohue (Eds.), *Sexual deviance: Theory, assessment, and treatment* (2nd ed.) (pp.571-610). New York: Guilford Press.

Kafka, M. P., & Hennon, J. (2002). A DSM IV Axis I comorbidity study of males (*n*=120) with paraphilias and paraphilia-related disorders. *Sexual Abuse: A Journal of Research and Treatment, 14*, 307–321.

Kenrick, D. T., Gutierres, S. E., & Goldberg, L. L. (1989). Influence of popular erotica on judgments of strangers and mates. *Journal of Experimental Social Psychology, 25*, 159–167.

Kilpatrick, J. (1996). From the mouths of victims: What victimization surveys tell us about sexual assault and sex offenders. Paper presented at the 15th Annual Research and Treatment Conference of the Association for the Treatment of Sexual Abusers. Chicago. Cited in W. L. Marshall, L. E. Marshall, G. A. Serran & Y. M. Fernandez (2006). *Treating sex offenders: An integrated approach* (p. 2). NY: Routledge, Taylor, & Francis Group.

Kinsey, A. C., Pomeroy, W. B., & Martin, C. E. (1948). *Sexual behavior in the human male.* Philadelphia: Saunders.

Knight, R. A., Prentky, R. A., & Cerce, D. (1994). The development, reliability, and validity of an inventory for the multidimensional assessment of sex and aggression. *Criminal Justice and Behavior, 21,* 72–94.

Knight, R. A., & Sims-Knight, J. E. (2003). The developmental antecedents of sexual coercion against women: Testing alternative hypotheses with structural equation modeling. In R. A. Prentky, E. S. Janus, & M. C. Seto (Eds.), *Sexually coercive behavior: Understanding and management* (pp. 72–85). New York: The New York Academy of Sciences.

Koss, M. P. (1992). The underdetection of rape: Are there differences in the victim's experience? *Psychology of Women Quarterly, 12,* 1–24.

Koss, M. P., & Gidyez, C. (1985). Sexual experiences survey: Reliability and validity. *Journal of Consulting and Clinical Psychology, 53,* 422–423.

Koss, M. P., Gidyez, C., & Wisniewski, N. (1987). The scope of rape: Incidence and prevalence of sexual aggression and victimization in a national sample of higher education students. *Journal of Clinical and Consulting Psychology, 55,* 162–170.

Koss, M. P., & Oros, C. J. (1982). Sexual experiences survey: A research instrument investigating sexual aggression and victimization. *Journal of Consulting and Clinical Psychology, 50,* 455–457.

Kutchinsky, B. (1991). Pornography and rape: Theory and practice? *International Journal of Law and Psychiatry, 14,* 47–64.

La Ford, J. Q. (2005). *Preventing sexual violence: How society should cope with sex offenders.* Washington, DC: American Psychological Association.

Lalumiere, M. L., Harris, G. T., Quinsey, V. L., & Rice, M. E. (2005). *The causes of rape: Understanding individual differences in male propensity for sexual aggression.* Washington, DC: American Psychological Association.

Langevin, R., Bain, J., Ben-Aron, M. H., Coulthard, R., Day, D., Handy, L., et al. (1985). Sexual aggression: Constructing a prediction equation. In R. Langevin (Ed.), *Erotic preference, gender identity, and aggression in men: New research studies* (pp. 39–76). Hillsdale, NJ: Lawrence Erlbaum and Associates.

Langevin, R., & Lang, R. A. (1990). Substance abuse among sex offenders. *Annals of Sex Research, 3,* 397–424.

Langstrom, N., & Hanson, R. K. (2006). High rates of sexual behavior in the general population: Correlates and predictors. *Archives of Sexual Behavior, 35,* 37–52.

Laumann, E. O., Gagnon, J. H., Michael, R. T., & Michaels, S. (1994). *The social organization of sexuality: Sexual practices in the United States.* Chicago: University of Chicago Press.

Laws, D. R. (1986). *Sexual deviance card sort.* Tampa, Fl: Florida Mental Health Institute.

Laws, D. R. (2008). The public health approach: A way forward. In D. R. Laws & W. T. O'Donohue (Eds.), *Sexual deviance: Theory, assessment, and treatment* (pp. 611–628). New York: Guilford Press.

Laws, D. R., & O'Donohue, W. T. (Eds.) (2008). *Sexual deviance: Theory, assessment, and treatment* (2nd ed.). New York: Guilford Press.

Laws, D. R., & Ward, T. (2006). When one size doesn't fit all: The reformulation of relapse prevention. In W. L. Marshall, Y. M. Fernandez, L. E. Marshall, & G. A. Serran (Eds.), *Sexual offender treatment: Controversial issues* (pp. 241–254). Chichester, UK: John Wiley & Sons.

Lazarus, R. S., & Folkman, S. (1984). *Stress, appraisal and coping.* New York: Guilford Press.

Lepper, M. R., Greene, D., & Nisbett, R. E. (1973). Undermining children's intrinsic interests with extrinsic reward: A test of the "overjustification" hypothesis. *Journal of Personality and Social Psychology, 28,* 129–137.

Levenson, J. S. (2004). Sexual predator civil commitment: A comparison of selected and released offenders. *International Journal of Offender Therapy and Comparative Criminology, 48,* 638–648.

Lightfoot, L. O., & Barbaree, H. E. (1993). The relationship between substance use and abuse and sexual offending in adolescents. In H. E. Barbaree &W. L. Marshall (Eds.), *The juvenile sex offender* (pp. 203–224). New York: Guilford Press.

Lisak, D., & Miller, P. M. (2002). Repeat rape and multiple offending among undetected rapists. *Violence and Victims, 17,* 73–84.

Lonsway, K. A. (1996). Preventing acquaintance rape through education: What do we know? *Psychology of Women Quarterly, 20,* 229–265.

Looman, J. (1999). Mood, conflict, and deviant sexual fantasies. In B. K. Schwartz (Ed.), *The sex offender: Theoretical advances, treating special populations and legal developments* (Vol. 3) (pp. 3.1–3.11). Kingston, NJ: Civic Research Institute.

Looman, J., Abracen, J., & Nicholaichuk, T. P. (2000). Recidivism among treated sexual offenders and matched controls. *Journal of Interpersonal Violence, 15,* 279–290.

Looman, J., & Marshall, W. L. (2005). Sexual arousal in rapists. *Criminal Justice and Behavior, 32,* 367–389.

MacCulloch, M. J., Snowden, P. R., Wood, P. J. W., & Mills, H. E. (1983). Sadistic fantasy, sadistic behavior and offending. *British Journal of Psychiatry, 143,* 20–29.

Macpherson, G. J. D. (2003). Predicting escalation in sexually violent recidivism: Use of the SVR-20 and PCL:SV to predict outcome with non-contact recidivists and contact recidivists. *Journal of Forensic Psychiatry and Psychology, 14,* 515–627.

Mahoney, M. J. (1974). *Cognitive and behavioral modification.* Cambridge, MA: Ballinger.

Malamuth, N. M. (1981). Rape proclivity among males. *Journal of Social Issues. 37,* 138–157.

Malamuth, N. M. (1989). The Attraction to Sexual Aggression Scale: Part two. *Journal of Sex Research, 26,* 324–354.

Malamuth, N. M. (2003). Criminal and noncriminal sexual aggressors: Integrating psychopathology in a hierarchical-mediational confluence model. In R. A. Prentky, E. S. Janus, & M. C. Seto (Eds.), *Sexually coercive behavior: Understanding and management* (Vol. 989) (pp. 33–58). New York: The New York Academy of Sciences.

Malamuth, N. M., Addison, T., & Koss, M. (2000). Pornography and sexual aggression: Are there reliable effects and can we understand them? *Annual Review of Sex Research, 11,* 26–91.

Malamuth, N. M., & Brown, L. M. (1994). Sexually aggressive men's perception of women's communications: Testing three explanations. *Journal of Personality and Social Psychology, 67,* 699–712.

Malamuth, N. M., & Check, J. V. P. (1980). Penile tumescence and perceptual responses to rape as a function of victim's perceived reactions. *Journal of Applied Social Psychology, 10,* 528–547.

Malamuth, N. M., & Check, J. V. P. (1981). The effects of mass media exposure on acceptance of violence against women: A field experiment. *Journal of Research in Personality, 15,* 436–446.

Malamuth, N. M., Heavy, C. L., & Linz, D. (1993). Predicting men's antisocial behavior against women: The interaction model of sexual aggression. In G. C. N. Hall, R. Hirshman, J. R. Graham, & M.S. Zaragoza (Eds.), *Sexual aggression: Issues in the etiology, assessment and treatment* (pp. 63–97). Washington, DC: Taylor & Francis.

Malamuth, N. M., Linz, D., Heavey, C. L., Barnes, G., & Acker, M. (1995). Characteristics of aggressors against women: Testing a model using a national sample of college students. *Journal of Consulting and Clinical Psychology, 59,* 670–681.

Mann, R. E., & Shingler, J. (2006). Schema-driven cognition in sexual offenders: Theory, assessment and treatment. In W. L. Marshall, Y. M. Fernandez, L. E. Marshall, & G. A. Serran (Eds.), *Sexual offender treatment: Controversial issues* (pp. 173–185). Chichester, UK: John Wiley & Sons Ltd.

Marolla, J., & Schully, D. (1986). Attitudes toward women, violence, and rape: A comparison of convicted rapists and other felons. *Deviant Behavior, 7,* 337–355.

Marques, J. K., Wiederanders, M., Day, D. M., Nelson, C., & van Ommeren, A. (2005). Effects of a relapse prevention program on sexual recidivism: Final results from California's Sex Offender Treatment and Evaluation Project (SOTEP). *Sexual Abuse: A Journal of Research and Treatment, 17,* 79–107.

Marshall, W. L. (1993). The role of attachments, intimacy and loneliness in the etiology and maintenance of sexual offending. *Sexual and Marital Therapy, 8,* 109-121.

Marshall, W. L. (1997a). Pedophilia: Psychopathology and theory. In D. R. Laws & W. O'Donohue (Eds.), *Handbook of sexual deviance: Theory and application* (pp. 152–174). New York: Guilford Press.

Marshall, W. L. (1997b). The relationship between self-esteem and deviant sexual arousal in nonfamilial child molesters. *Behavior Modification, 12,* 86–96.

Marshall, W. L. (2002). Development of empathy. In Fernandez, Y. (Ed.), *In their shoes: Examining the issue of empathy and its place in the treatment of offenders* (pp. 36–52). Oklahoma City: Wood 'N' Barnes Publishing & Distribution.

Marshall, W. L. (2006a). Appraising treatment outcome with sexual offenders. In W. L. Marshall, Y. M. Fernandez, L. E.Marshall, & G. A. Serran (Eds.), *Sexual offender treatment: Controversial issues* (pp. 255–273). Chichester, UK: John Wiley & Sons Ltd.

Marshall, W. L. (2006b). Diagnostic problems with sexual offenders. In W. L. Marshall, Y. M. Fernandez, L. E.Marshall, & G. A. Serran (Eds.), *Sexual offender treatment: Controversial issues* (pp. 33–43). Chichester, UK: John Wiley & Sons Ltd.

Marshall, W. L., Anderson, D., & Champagne, F. (1997). Self-esteem and its relationship to sexual offending. *Psychology, Crime & Law, 3,* 81–106.

Marshall, W. L., & Barbaree, H. E. (1990). An integrated theory of the etiology of sexual offending. In W. L. Marshall, D. R. Laws, & H. E. Barbaree (Eds.), *Handbook of sexual assault: Issues, theories, and treatment of the offender (pp. 257–275).* New York: Plenum Press.

Marshall, W. L., Fernandez, Y. M., Serran, G. A., Mulloy, R., Thorton, D., Mann, R. E., et al. (2003). Process variables in the treatment of sexual offenders: A review of the literature. *Aggression and Violent Behavior, 8,* 205–234.

Marshall, W. L., Kennedy, P., & Yates, P. (2002). Issues concerning the reliability and validity of the diagnosis as applied in prison settings. *Sexual Abuse: A Journal of Research and Treatment, 14,* 310–311.

Marshall, W. L., Kennedy, P., Yates, P., & Serran, G. A. (2002). Diagnosing sexual sadism in sexual offenders: Reliability across diagnosticians. *International Journal of Offender Therapy and Comparative Criminology, 46,* 668–76.

Marshall, W. L., Marshall, L. E., Serran, G. A., & Fernandez, Y. M. (2006). *Treating sexual offenders: An integrated approach.* New York: Routledge, Taylor & Francis Group.

Marshall, W. L., Seidman, B. T., & Barbaree, H. E. (1991). The effects of prior exposure to erotic and nonerotic stimulie on the rape index. *Annals of Sex Research, 4,* 209–220.

Marshall, W. L., & Yates, P. M. (2005). Comment on Maillox et al.'s (2003) study: "Dosage of treatment of sexual offenders: Are we overprescribing?" *International Journal of Offender Treatment and Comparative Criminology, 49,* 221–224.

Martin, D. J., Garske, J. P., & Davis, M. K. (2000). Relation of the therapeutic alliance with outcome and other variables: A meta-analytic review. *Journal of Consulting and Clinical Psychology, 68,* 438–450.

Marziali, E., & Alexander, L. (1991). The power of the therapeutic relationship. *American Journal of Orthopsychiatry, 61,* 383–391.

McGuff, R., Gitlin, D., & Enderlin, D. (1996). Clients' and therapists' confidence and attendance at planned individual therapy sessions. *Psychological Reports, 79,* 537–538.

Miller, W. R. (1983). Motivational interviewing with problem drinkers. *Behavioral Psychotherapy, 1,* 147–172.

Miller, W. R., Benefield, R. G., & Tonigan, J. S. (1993). Enhancing motivation for change in problem drinking: A controlled comparison of two therapist styles. *Journal of Consulting and Clinical Psychology, 61,* 455–461.

Miller, W. R., & Mount, K. A. (2001). A small study of training in motivational interviewing: Does one workshop change clinician and client behavior? *Behavioral and Cognitive Psychotherapy, 29,* 457–471.

Miller, W. R., & Rollnick, S. (2002). *Motivational interviewing: Preparing people to change addictive behavior.* New York: Guilford Press.

Miller, W. R., Taylor, C. A., & West, J. C. (1980). Focused versus broad-spectrum behavior therapy for problem drinkers. *Journal of Consulting and Clinical Psychology, 48,* 590–601.

Miller, W. R., Yahne, C. E., Moyers, T. B., Martinez, J., & Pirritano, M. (2004). A randomized trail of methods to help clinicians learn motivational interviewing. *Journal of Consulting and Clinical Psychology, 72,* 1050–1062.

Muehlenhard, C. L., & Linton, M. A. (1987). Date rape and sexual aggression in dating situations: Incidence and risk factors. *Journal of Counseling Psychology, 34,* 186–196.

Murphy, W. D., & Barbaree, H. E. (1994). *Assessments of sex offenders by measures of erectile response: Psychometric properties and decision making.* Brandon, VT: The Safer Society Press.

Nichols, H. R., & Molinder, I. (1984). *Multiphasic Sex Inventory.* Tacoma, WA: Authors.

Nicolaichuk, T., Gordon, A., Gu, D., & Wong, S. (2000). Outcome of an institutional sexual offender treatment program: A comparison between treated and matched untreated offenders. *Sexual Abuse: A Journal of Research and Treatment, 12,* 139–153.

Norris, J., George, W. H., Davis, K. C., Martell, J., & Leonesio, R. J. (1999). Alcohol and hypermasculinity as determinants of men's empathic response to violent pornography. *Journal of Interpersonal Violence, 14,* 683–700.

O'Donohue, W. T., Regev, L. G., & Hagstrom, A. (2000). Problems with the DSM-IV diagnosis of pedophilia. *Sex Abuse: A Journal of Research and Treatment, 12,* 95–105.

Orlinsky, D. E., Grawe, K., & Parks, B. K. (1994). Process and outcome in psychotherapy. In A. E. Bergin & S. L. Garfield (Eds.), *Handbook of psychotherapy and behavior change* (4th ed.) (270–376). New York: John Wiley & Sons, Ltd.

Padesky, C. A. (1994). Schema change processes in cognitive therapy. *Clinical Psychology and Psychotherapy, 1,* 267–278.

Parks, K. A., & Miller, B. A. (1997). Bar victimization of women. *Psychology of Women Quarterly, 21,* 509–525.

Patterson, G. R., & Forgatch, M. S. (1985). Therapist behavior as a determinant for client noncompliance: A paradox for the behavior modifier. *Journal of Consulting and Clinical Psychology, 53,* 846–851.

Peters, S. D., Wyatt, G. E., & Finkelhor, D. (1986). Prevalence. In D. Finkelhor (Ed.), *A sourcebook in child sexual abuse* (pp. 15–59). Beverly Hills, CA: Sage Publications.

Piatogorsky, A., & Hinshaw, S. P. (2004). Psychopathic traits in boys with and without attention-deficit/hyperactivity disorder: Concurrent and longitudinal correlates. *Journal of Abnormal Child Psychology, 32,* 535–550.

Pithers, W. D. (1999). Empathy: Definition, enhancement, and relevance to the treatment of sexual abusers. *Journal of Interpersonal Violence, 14,* 257–284.

Prentky, R. A., & Burgess, A. W. (2000). *Forensic management of sexual offenders.* New York: Kluver Academic/Plenum.

Prochaska, J., & Norcross, J. (2004). Systems of psychotherapy: *A transtheoretical analysis* (5th ed.). New York: Wadsworth.

Prochaska, J., & Prochaska, J. M. (1991). Why don't people change? Why don't continents move? *Journal of Psychotherapy Integration, 9,* 83–102.

Proeve, M., & Howells, K. (2005). Shame and guilt in child molesters. In W. L. Marshall, Y. M. Fernandez, L. E. Marshall, & G. A. Serran (Eds.), *Sexual offender treatment: Controversial issues* (pp. 125–139). Chichester, UK: John Wiley & Sons, Ltd.

Proulx, J., Blais, E., & Beauregard, E. (2006). Sadistic sexual aggressors. In W. L. Marshall, Y. M. Fernandez, L. E. Marshall, G. A. Serran (Eds.), *Sexual offender treatment: Controversial issues* (pp. 61–77). Chichester, UK: John Wiley & Sons, Ltd.

Quimette, P. C. (1997). Psychopathology and sexual aggression in nonincarcerated men. *Violence and Victims, 12,* 389–395.

Quimette, P. C., & Riggs, D. (1998). Testing a mediational model of sexually aggressive behavior in nonincarcerated perpetrators. *Violence and Victims, 12,* 117–130.

Quinsey, V. L., Harris, G. T., Rice, M. E., & Cormier, C. A. (1998). *Violent offenders: Appraising and managing risk.* Washington, DC: American Psychological Association.

Rabavilas, A., Boulougouris, J., & Perissaki, C. (1979). Therapist qualities related to outcome with exposure in vivo in neurotic patients. *Journal of Behavioral Therapy and Experimental Psychiatry, 10,* 293–294.

Rabinowitz, S. R., Firestone, P., Bradford, J. M., & Greenberg, D. M. (2002). Prediction of recidivism in exhibitionists: Psychological, phallometric, and offense factors. *Sexual Abuse: A Journal of Research and Treatment, 14,* 329–347.

Rada, R. T. (1978). *Clinical aspects of the rapist.* New York: Grune and Stratton.

Raymond, N. C., Coleman, E., Ohlerking, F., Christianson, G. A., & Minor, M. (1999). Psychiatric comorbidity in pedophilic sex offenders. *American Journal of Psychiatry, 156,* 786–788.

Ready v. Commonwealth, 824 N.E. 2d 474 (Mass. Ct. App. 2005).

Rice, M. E., & Harris, G. T. (1997). Cross-validation and extension of the Violence Risk Appraisal Guide for child molesters and rapists. *Law and Human Behavior, 21,* 231–241.

Richardson, D, & Campbell, J. L. (1982). Alcohol and rape: The effect of alcohol on attributions of blame for rape. *Personality and Social Psychology Bulletin, 8,* 468–476.

Roizen, J. (1997). Epidemiological issues in alcohol-related violence. In M. Galanter (Ed.), *Recent developments in alcoholism* (pp. 7–40). New York: Plenum Press.

Russel, D. (1990). *Rape in marriage.* New York: Macmillan.

Ryan, V. L., & Gizynski, M. N. (1971). Behavior therapy in retrospect: Patients' feelings and their behavior therapies. *Journal of Consulting and Clinical Psychology, 37,* 1–9.

Safran, J. D., & Segal, Z. V. (1990). *Interpersonal process in cognitive therapy.* New York: Basic Books.

Salter, A. C. (1988). *Treating child sex offenders and victims: A practical guide.* Newbury Park, CA: Sage Publications.

Saltzman, C., Luetgert, M. J., Roth, C. H., Creaser, J., & Howard, L. (1976). Formation of therapeutic relationship: Experiences during the initial phase of psychotherapy as predictors of treatment duration and outcome. *Journal of Consulting and Clinical Psychology, 44,* 546–555.

Saunders, M. (1999). Clients' assessments of the affective environment of the psychotherapy session: Relationship to session quality and treatment effectiveness. *Journal of Clinical Psychology, 55,* 597–605.

Schaap, C., Brennun, I., Schindler, L., & Hoogduin, K. (1993). *The therapeutic relationship in behavioral psychotherapy.* Chichester, England: John Wiley & Sons, Ltd.

Schewe, P., & O'Donohue, W. (1993). Rape prevention: Methodological problems and new directions. *Clinical Psychology Review, 13,* 667–682.

Schewe, P., & O'Donohue, W. (1996). Rape prevention with high-risk males: Short-term outcome of two interventions. *Archives of Sexual Behavior, 25,* 455–471.

Schwartz, B. K., & Cellini, H. R. (1995). Female sex offenders. In B. K. Schwartz & H. R. Cellini (Eds.), *The sex offender: Corrections, treatment, and legal practice* (Vol. 1) (pp. 5.2–5.20). Kingston, NJ: Civic Research Institute.

Schweitzer, R., & Dwyer, J. (2003). Sex crime recidivism: Evaluation of a sexual offender treatment program. *Journal of Interpersonal Violence, 18,* 1292–1310.

Scott, R. L., & Tetreault, L. A. (1987). Attitudes of rapists and other violent offenders toward women. *Journal of Social Psychology, 127,* 375–380.

Seligman, L. (1990). *Selecting effective treatments.* San Francisco: Jossey-Bass.

Senn, C. Y., Desmarais, S., Verberg, N., & Wood, E. (2000). Predicting coercive and sexual behavior across the lifespan in a random sample of Canadian men. *Journal of Social and Personal Relationships, 17,* 95–113.

Serran, G. A., & Marshall, L. E. (2005). Coping and mood in sexual offending. In W. L., Marshall, Y. M. Fernandez, L. E. Marshall, & G. A. Serran (Eds.), *Sexual offender treatment: Controversial issues* (pp. 109–126). Chichester, UK: John Wiley & Sons, Ltd.

Seto, M. C. (2008). *Pedophilia and sexual offending against children: Theory, assessment, and intervention.* Washington, DC: American Psychological Association.

Seto, M. C., & Lalumiere, M. L. (2001). A brief screening scale to identify pedophilic interests among child molesters. *Sexual Abuse: A Journal of Research and Treatment, 13,* 15–25.

Seto, M. C., Marc, A., & Barbaree, H. E. (2001). The role of pornography in the etiology of sexual aggression. *Aggression and Violent Behavior, 6,* 35–53.

Smallbone, S. W. (2005). Attachment insecurity as a predisposing and precipitating factor for sexual offending by young people. In W. L. Marshall, Y. M. Fernandez, L. E. Marshall, & G. A. Serran (Eds.), *Sexual offender treatment: Controversial issues* (pp. 93–107). Chichester, UK: John Wiley & Sons, Ltd.

Smallbone, S. W., & Dadds, M. R. (1998). Childhood sexual attachment and adult attachment in incarcerated adult male sex offenders. *Journal of Interpersonal Violence, 13,* 555–573.

Smith, G., & Fischer, L. (1999). Assessment of juvenile sexual offenders: Reliability and validity of the Abel Assessment for interest in paraphilias. *Sexual Abuse: A Journal of Research and Treatment, 11,* 207–216.

Snyder, H. N. (2000). *Sexual assault of young children as reported to law enforcement: Victim, incident, and offender characteristics* (NCJ 182990). Washington, DC: National Center for Juvenile Justice.

Spitzer, R. L., Williams, J. B. W., Gibbon, M., & First, M. (1987). *Structured Clinical Interview for DSM-III-R.* Washington, DC: American Psychiatric Press.

Steele, C. M., & Josephs, R. A. (1990). Alcohol myopia: its prized and dangerous effects. *American Psychologist, 45,* 921–933.

Stinson, J. D., Sales, B. D., & Becker, J. V. (2008). *Sex offending: Causal theories to inform research, prevention, and treatment.* Washington, DC: American Psychological Association.

Strupp, H. H. (1980). Success and failure in time-limited psychotherapy: A systematic comparison of cases. *Archives of General Psychiatry, 37,* 595–603.

Strupp, H. H., & Hadley, S. W. (1979). Specific versus nonspecific factors of psychotherapy. *Archives of General Psychiatry, 36,* 1125–1136.

Testa, M. (2002). The impact of men's alcohol consumption on perpetration of sexual aggression. *Clinical Psychology Review, 22,* 1239–1263.

Thornton, D. (2002). Constructing and testing a framework for dynamic risk assessment. *Sexual Abuse: A Journal of Research and Treatment, 14,* 139–154.

Thornton, D., Beech, A., R., & Marshall, W. L. (2004). Pretreatment self-esteem and posttreatment sexual recidivism. *International Journal of Offender Therapy and Comparative Criminology, 48,* 587–599.

Tjaden, P., & Thoennes, N. (1998). *Prevalence, incidence, and consequences of violence against women: Findings from the national violence against women survey* (NCJ 172837), Washington, DC: US Department of Justice.

Tjaden, P. & Thoennes, N. (2000). Prevalence and consequences of male-to-female and female-to-male intimate partner violence as measured by the national violence against women survey. *Violence Against Women, 6,* 142–161.

Ullman, S. E., Karabatsos, G., & Koss, M. P. (1999). Alcohol and sexual aggression in a national sample of college men. *Psychology of Women Quarterly, 23,* 673–689.

United States Department of Justice. (2006). *Crime in the United States, 2004.* Washington, DC: US Government Printing Office.

United States v. Weber, F.3d, 06, Cal. Daily Op. Serv. 5211 (9th Cir. June 20, 2006).

Walker, W. D. (1997). *Patterns in sexual offending.* Unpublished doctoral dissertation, Queen's University, Kingston.

Walker, W. D., Rowe, R. C., & Quinsey, V. L. (1993). Authoritarianism and sexual aggression. *Journal of Personality and Social Psychology, 65,* 1036–1045.

Ward, T. (2002). Good lives and the rehabilitation of offenders: Promises and problems. *Aggression and Violent Behavior: A Review Journal, 7,* 513–528.

Ward, T., & Beech, A. R. (2008). An integrated theory of sexual offending. In R. D. Laws & W. T. O'Donohue (Eds.), *Sexual deviance: Theory, assessment, and treatment* (pp. 21–36). New York: Guilford Press.

Ward, T., Hudson, S. M., Marshall, W. L., & Siegert, R. J. (1995). Attachment style and intimacy deficits in sex offenders: A theoretical framework. *Sex Abuse: A Journal of Research and Treatment, 7,* 317–335.

Ward, T, & Keenan, T. (1999). Child molesters' implicit theories. *Journal of Interpersonal Violence, 14,* 821–838.

Ward, T., & Stewart, C. A. (2003). Criminogenic needs or human needs: A theoretical critique. *Psychology, Crime & Law, 9,* 125–143.

Weaver, J. B., Masland, J. L., & Zillmann, D. (1984). Effect of erotica on young men's aesthetic perception of their female sexual partners. *Perceptual and Motor Skills, 58,* 929–930.

Webster, S. D., Bowers, L. E., Mann, R. E., & Marshall, W. L. (2005). Developing empathy in sexual offenders: The value of offense re-enactments. *Sexual Abuse: A Journal of Research and Treatment, 17,* 63–77.

White, J. W., & Smith, P. H. (2004). Sexual assault perpetration and reperpetration: From adolescence to young adulthood. *Criminal Justice and Behavior, 31,* 182–202.

Wilson, R. J., & Picheca, J. E. (2005). Circles of support and accountability: Engaging the community in sexual offender management. In B. K. Schwartz (Ed.), *The sex offender: Theoretical advances, treating special populations and legal developments* (Vol. 5) (pp. 13.1–13.21). Kingston, NJ: Civic Research Institute.

Witt, P. H., & Conroy, M. A. (2009). *Evaluation of sexually violent predators.* New York: Oxford University Press.

Yalom, D. D., & Lieberman, M. A. (1971). A study of encounter group casualties. *Archives of General Psychiatry, 25,* 16–30.

Yates, E., Barbaree, H. E., & Marshall, W. L. (1984). Anger and deviant sexual arousal. *Behavior Therapy, 15,* 287–294.

Young, J. E. (1990). *Cognitive therapy for personality disorder: A Schema-focused approach.* Sarasota, FL: Professional Resources Press.

Zillmann, D., & Bryant, J. (1988). Pornography's impact on sexual satisfaction. *Journal of Applied Social Psychology, 18,* 438–453.

Zucker, P. J., Worthington, E. L., & Forsyth, D. R. (1985). Increasing empathy through participation in structured groups. Some attributional evidence. *Human Relations, 38,* 247–255.

Zurbriggen, E. I. (2000). Social motives and cognitive power-sex associations: Predictors of aggressive sexual behavior. *Journal of Personality and Social Psychology, 78,* 559–581.